What people are saying about . . .

Good News for Those Trying Harder

"The most readable, realistic, and biblically right-on discussion of spiritual formation I've read in a long time. Try hard and you'll feel tired or proud. Get real and you'll trust Christ as never before. In a nutshell, that's the message Kraft beautifully unpacks. I felt a weight lift as I read it, and you will too."

Dr. Larry Crabb, speaker, founder of NewWay Ministries, and author of *Shattered Dreams* and *The Pressure's Off*

"Alan Kraft has charted a road map that points, in very clear and practical ways, to a pathway of *hope* and *help* for Christians who are tired of stumbling and fumbling—tired of the treadmill of weariness with efforts that end in discouragement and defeat. If you want to understand how the joyous and dynamic life of a true disciple of Jesus can be experienced, here's the handbook."

Dr. Jack W. Hayford, president of International Foursquare Churches, chancellor of The King's College and Seminary, and founding pastor of The Church On The Way

"God has a way of bringing us to the end of our resources in order that we may discover His. Sadly, many resist this brokenness, but it is the key to the victorious and what God intended to be the 'normal' Christian life, which is 'Christ in you the hope of glory.' Alan has discovered what it means to let the life of Christ live through him and to let it happen rather than struggle to make it happen. I highly recommend this book for every Christian pilgrim who wants to live a liberated, righteous, and fruitful life by faith in the power of the Holy Spirit."

Dr. Neil T. Anderson, founder and president
of Freedom in Christ Ministries

"In a very honest and compelling way, Alan Kraft shows us why believers still need the gospel every day. *Good News for Those Trying Harder* should help many people get off the performance treadmill in their relationship with God. I highly recommend it."

Dr. Jerry Bridges, author of *The Pursuit of Holiness*

"God speaks through Alan Kraft, and his book made my 'must read' list. This message is for every Christian, but especially for pastors and ministry leaders who sometimes serve out of their own efforts instead of relying on God's Spirit. This book brought me to tears more than once. Read it and let God refresh your faith."

Alan Nelson, executive editor of *Rev! Magazine*
and author of *Me to We*

"It is rare that I have gained as much helpful insight for my spiritual life in one book. Alan's illustrations and practical advice were striking. Many of his ideas were so thought provoking that I would lay down the book and pray. The entire book was refreshing and caused me to relax, sit back, and ponder the beauty of Christ."

Bill Hull, author of *Choose the Life:*
Exploring a Faith That Embraces Discipleship

"I sure wish more pastors were willing to be as honest and forthright as Alan Kraft. Too often the biblical realities of our spiritual battle are hidden behind clichés and facades designed to make us—and even God—somehow look better. As a result, the real message of the gospel gets lost. Alan calls us to get off the treadmill of fleshly effort disguised as godly discipline and scurry back to the power of the simple gospel; a gospel that is not just the starting point, but the context of the entire race."

Dr. Larry Osborne, author and pastor of North Coast Church

"Alan Kraft has captured in a fresh way the essence of gospel transformation, hearing the melody of brokenness and faith as we practice living in His presence. I was refreshed and renewed as I read this book."

Dr. William J. Hamel, president of the
Evangelical Free Church of America

"Many who once took their faith seriously are either considering (or are currently) walking away from the church. Alan Kraft's gospel-clarifying and faith-restoring book addresses the core issue for this exodus and shows the path back to authentic faith. I love Alan's heart and honesty. Read, understand, and apply the truth in these pages. If you do, it will change everything."

Dan Webster, founder of Authentic Leadership, Inc.

"For those of us who find ourselves cranky, sour, angry, or cynical while trying to do God's work, Alan Kraft eases our burden. Instead of trying to please God, Alan leads us to trust God. And delight in Him. This is a freeing book that redefines what it means to live by faith. Just what I needed."

Marshall Shelley, editor of *Leadership Journal*

"If you have called yourself a Christian for longer than a day, this book is for you. Alan has courageously spoken clear truths for all of us who were raised and convinced that for every problem in our lives, trying harder is the answer. Few books have truly impacted me like this one. Without a doubt, this will be an annual read for me."

Dr. Chuck Stecker, author, national speaker, and president of A Chosen Generation

"Good timing, Alan! This book has come into my hands precisely at a time when I am being made painfully aware that my own zeal and determination are insufficient to touch kingdom fullness. Once again I am throwing myself upon the mercy of a God who is committed to working in us according to *HIS* zeal and determination (Phil. 2:13). And that's what this book is about—celebrating the power of God to do in us what we cannot do for ourselves. Alan's unfolding insights will skillfully guide you into a fresh discovery of the true freedom of the gospel."

Bob Sorge, author of *Secrets of the Secret Place*

"Sadly, many in the Christian community seem to know little about grace. They may be quick to say they're *saved* by grace, but they are unclear about *living* by grace. Grace isn't just the first square on the walking-with-God board game. Grace isn't just amazing for the wretched sinner. Grace is amazing from the day we're born again to the day we meet Christ at the end of our journey. *Alan Kraft gets it!* Alan's book is liberating and transformational because grace is liberating and transformational."

Dr. Gary D. Kinnaman, pastor and author of *Angels Dark and Light*

From those who were trying harder …

"I spent so much of my life as a Pharisee until Jesus showed me the depth of my own depravity and how deeply I needed Him. Jesus offers a yoke that is easy, a burden that is light…. Finally, life in the fullest possible way. Hallelujah!"

Dave

"We had always believed that our actions were the key to God's acceptance. We have gradually begun to see through new covenant eyes that the gospel is NOT 'Jesus plus my good works,' or 'Jesus plus the Sabbath,' or 'Jesus plus anything'! We are discovering the marvelous simplicity and awesome power of the true gospel of Jesus Christ."

Joe and Bev

"For over twenty years, my wife and I were in a high-performance ministry mode. I ended up bitter, disillusioned, and burned out. My wife was exhausted…. Over a several-month period, our lives were dramatically changed. We had hope again and knew that this was what we were missing…. Jesus really is our Savior from first to last, and we're excited that He deeply desires to manifest His life through us. This is truly good news!"

Boak

Good News
for Those
Trying Harder

Good News
for Those
Trying Harder

Alan Kraft

David C Cook®

transforming lives together

GOOD NEWS FOR THOSE TRYING HARDER
Published by David C. Cook
4050 Lee Vance View
Colorado Springs, CO 80918 U.S.A.

David C. Cook Distribution Canada
55 Woodslee Avenue, Paris, Ontario, Canada N3L 3E5

David C. Cook U.K., Kingsway Communications
Eastbourne, East Sussex BN23 6NT, England

David C. Cook and the graphic circle C logo
are registered trademarks of Cook Communications Ministries.

The Web site addresses recommended throughout this book are offered as a
resource to you. These Web sites are not intended in any way to be or imply an
endorsement on the part of David C. Cook, nor do we vouch for their content.

All Scripture quotations, unless otherwise noted, are taken from the *Holy
Bible, New International Version*®. *NIV*®. Copyright © 1973, 1978, 1984
by International Bible Society. Used by permission of Zondervan. All rights
reserved. Scripture quotations marked NASB are taken from the *New American
Standard Bible*, © Copyright 1960, 1995 by The Lockman Foundation. Used
by permission. All italics in Scripture are added by the author for emphasis.

The One Year Bible copyright © 1985, 1986, 1987, 1989, 1991, 1996, 2004.
By Tyndale House Publishers. Used by permission. All rights reserved.
One Year is a registered trademark of Tyndale House Publishers, Inc.

LCCN 2008906912
ISBN 978-1-4347-9940-1

The Team: John Blase and Jack Campbell

Cover Photo: Veer, Inc.
Author Photo: Robin Watson

Printed in the United States of America
First Edition 2008

1 2 3 4 5 6 7 8 9 10

073008

To Raylene
My best friend

Contents

Acknowledgments

My heart is filled with gratitude toward so many who encouraged me in this endeavor, offered helpful feedback about the writing, and prayed (and are praying!) for this message to go far beyond the walls of Christ Community Church.

Special thanks …

To Raylene, whose continual encouragement, patience, and prayers helped make this dream possible.

To my incredible children—Erin, Joel, Caleb, and Joshua—whose dancing, laughing, bouncing, wrestling, and hugging continually reminded me not to take this project too seriously.

To so many friends, who at various times offered helpful feedback in the entire writing process: Phil Grizzle, Deanne Helmboldt, Stacey Campbell, Bruce Hoppe, Jasona and Doug Brown, Joe Smeltzer, Bob Putman, Willie Noll, David Staff, Joe Chaffin, Boak and Brenda Desmond, Scott and Betsy Kraft, Lynn Jeffers, Steve Bryan, Brian Mavis, and Eric Swanson.

To Bob Bever, who continually believed in the value of this message, helped open doors for it to be published, and often talked me through some discouraging moments in the journey.

To Shane Sunn, whose tenacity about the gospel helped open my eyes to see it in a new way.

To John Blase, my editor, whose encouragement helped me keep going and whose input made the communicating of this message significantly better.

To my dear friends and fellow journeyers in the gospel at Christ Community Church, whose wholehearted receptivity to and embracing of this message inspired me to put it into writing.

My heart is filled with gratitude toward all of you and to my incredible Savior, who is helping me hear the glorious melody of the gospel.

Introduction

When I was growing up, a friend of the family owned what was considered to be the state-of-the-art exercise equipment of the day. You may remember it. It consisted of a six-inch-wide belt that was connected to a machine. To exercise, you would put the belt around the back of your waist, turn the machine on, and let it jiggle your body. It was great fun for us kids; however, it didn't do much for any adult trying to get healthy—except perhaps cause temporary dizziness. While the prevailing wisdom of the day believed that movement of this sort would promote physical health, we now know the truth: Jiggling doesn't make anyone healthier or stronger.

In many ways, that exercise machine is a picture of the Christianity that many people are pursuing and promoting. The prevailing spiritual wisdom of the day seems to assert that movement results in health. As long as you stay busy with spiritual activities, your spiritual strength will grow. As long as you work hard to please God, you will mature. It sounds reasonable enough. In fact, it was the spiritual growth path I pursued for several years. However, what many Christians and I are discovering is that spiritual jiggling doesn't seem to accomplish the objective of spiritual maturity. Trying harder to follow God doesn't work. It doesn't seem to make us any less sinful.

Instead, it just makes us tired and increasingly disillusioned with the state of our spiritual lives.

There is good news, however. Trying harder was never God's spiritual growth plan for us. God has given us an entirely different pathway into the life He desires for us to experience. This book is a description of that pathway. In many respects, it is a picture of my own journey—off a twenty-five-year-long treadmill of spiritual performance and into the transforming ocean of God's purposes and presence. I invite you to join me in this journey.

This is a book for the spiritual seeker who longs to discover the nature of authentic spirituality. It's a book for the sincere Christ-follower who is busy with activity but inwardly weary of trying harder. And finally, it's a book for Christian pastors and leaders who long to help the people they serve more deeply experience life in Christ but feel as if something is missing. I pray that you will read with an open heart and be transformed by the experience.

Let me offer one suggestion: Don't hurry through this material. The goal is not as much about getting information as it is about experiencing transformation—changing the way you think about and experience the spiritual life. Some of the concepts may be a significant paradigm shift from what you have thought for years, so take your time. Prayerfully process what you are reading. There are a few reflection questions at the end of each chapter to give you opportunity to do just that. You may want to invite a friend to join you in this journey.

The ultimate objective is Jesus. May He use this book to help you more deeply experience Him.

❋ ❋ ❋

*Heavenly Father, You know the people reading
these words right now. You know their hearts,
their struggles, and their longing for a deeper experience
with You. Grant them the desires of their hearts as
they interact with and process the thoughts and ideas
in this book. Open their spiritual eyes to see the specific
things You long to speak into their souls—truths about the
depth of their need for You and the incredible Savior
that You are. I pray for a fullness of freedom and
joy in You that spills over into every facet of their lives.
In the name of Jesus, amen.*

Chapter One

The Struggle to Make It Work

"At this point I feel that I am more than ready to abandon my faith and commitment to Christ.... I have tried very hard to grow closer to God by having daily quiet times of Bible reading and prayer to spend time with Him, attending Bible college to better understand His Word, memorizing hundreds of Bible verses that the Holy Spirit might use them as a sword in spiritual battle, serving in several ministries so God could use me to accomplish His will, attempting to love others as Jesus would so that His name would be glorified, striving for obedience, making disciples, baptizing, fasting, praying in the Spirit, evangelizing, forsaking the world and holding back nothing, and following Him with complete faith. It all seems to be worthless. I tried so hard, but nothing really happened."

I was stunned as I read those words, written to me by a youth leader in our church. Darrin was a college senior who modeled a strong commitment to Christ. Well-versed in Scripture and faithful in his ministry to our high school youth, he was the epitome of spiritual maturity. And yet, there I was, reading this twelve-page document in which he articulated the reasons for recently deciding to abandon his faith. I was shell-shocked.

I met with Darrin soon after, and we talked specifically about several of his expressed concerns, many of which were faith struggles most all Christians have at one time or another—questions about why God allows suffering and how we know the Bible is true. But as I later processed this situation, it became clear the root of Darrin's faith struggle was actually much deeper than theological questions.

He was tired. He was tired of a Christianity that wasn't working. For years he had diligently pursued the spiritual growth path regularly encouraged by most Christ-followers. He had faithfully practiced spiritual disciplines like daily quiet times and Scripture memorization. He was actively involved in ministry and sharing his faith. He was busy doing what Christians are supposed to do but was increasingly troubled by questions simmering in the back of his mind: Why isn't this working? Why is this not really changing me or anyone around me? Why is this not bringing joy to my life?

Darrin was too ashamed to admit to anyone his feelings of doubt and disillusionment. He was able to keep up the spiritual game face … for a while at least. Finally, in his darkness of soul, he came to the only conclusion he could see at the time: Renounce your faith. Stop trying to do this Christian thing because it's not working. Ironically, I believe God had Darrin right where He wanted him—utterly discouraged and disillusioned with his own efforts, so that he might embrace a completely different approach to spirituality—the spiritual life God had in mind for him all along.

Nearly a year after his supposed abandonment of Christianity, Darrin stood in front of our church body, sharing the story of his initial renunciation and his more recent reaffirmation of his faith. As I listened to Darrin that morning, it became clear to me he had never truly renounced his faith in Christ. What he had abandoned was a Christianity rooted in self-effort, trying hard to measure up—which is no Christianity at all. Darrin's spiritual crisis opened a door for authentic transformation—the very thing that many sincere Christians, like Darrin, are longing for yet missing.

Avis Spirituality

In 1962, Avis was a relatively unprofitable company with only 11 percent of the car rental business in the United States. That year it launched an advertising campaign in which it relentlessly asserted what distinguished it as a company: We Try Harder. Within four years, Avis had tripled its market share to 35 percent. For many Christians, the Avis approach to business success becomes the fundamental approach to spiritual success—just try harder. After initially receiving Christ, we begin living our lives with an ever-growing list of the things that please God coupled with an inner drive to try hard to do those things.

This describes my early years as a Christian: earnest, devout, disciplined. I remember my routine as a college student involved fasting once a week, having daily devotional times, and regularly memorizing large portions of Scripture—none of which is bad in and of itself. For me, however, I was too spiritually busy to recognize how dry my soul was becoming. My relationship with God was wooden and mechanical as I earnestly focused on one objective:

trying very hard to please God by doing the things Christians are supposed to do.

This approach can look quite spiritual to those around us; however, it's often rooted in a soul deficiency, a deeply held inner conviction that our worth as Christians is dependent upon *our* ability to perform and succeed. Behind this spiritual facade is a heart desperately attempting to get God to love us more by doing the "shoulds." Ultimately, our obedience is rooted in guilt and fear, not freedom. Can you relate to this? Does your spiritual life boil down to how you can do a better job pleasing God? If so, I'd like you to consider the possibility that the spiritual path you are on may not result in the kind of real transformation you long for.

From Avis to Apathy

Often many Christ-followers, like Darrin, unintentionally find themselves in a place of *spiritual disillusionment.* After being on the "trying harder" spiritual growth path for several months or years, we eventually begin to experience a nagging feeling that something is not right. Frequently this manifests itself as a weariness of soul that has us wondering how long we can keep this up. The spiritual to-do lists offered in sermons and books that previously motivated and energized us now exhaust. We know we haven't mastered last week's list, and the thought of a longer list feels overwhelming. The words "spiritual failure" are continually whispered to our souls, but we're afraid to admit it to anyone else because they all seem to be doing okay. In response to this nagging feeling, we often settle into a place of passive resignation. Spiritual apathy. Like Darrin, we aren't *really* interested in *renouncing* Christ, but our motivation to live for Him is waning. We go through the motions of church and spiritual activity, but we're inwardly empty. Surely this is not what Jesus meant by life abundant.

In my own journey, this disillusionment and weariness of soul eventually surfaced at a time when life was going great. The church was growing; things were happening. I was invincible, or so I thought … until that moment when, out of the blue, I experienced my first anxiety attack—cold sweat, pounding heart, feeling as if the walls were closing in on me and I couldn't escape. It lasted for just a few minutes but felt like an eternity. I didn't know what was happening to me. I thought I *might* be losing my mind but was *certain* I was going to lose my job—which only increased my anxiety. In the midst of my struggle, I went to see a counselor who helped me uncover the underlying drivenness in my soul—a desperate need to be affirmed through success. Anxiety was God's tool to get my attention and help me see that something was not right in my relationship with Him. Whatever God's method, whether it be an overwhelming sense of failure or fear, the disillusionment is real. Maybe this describes you right now. On the outside, you are busy and look like you have it all together, but on the inside you know something is not right. You feel stuck. Your soul is tired of trying harder to please God and always feeling that you fall short. Perhaps you have thought about giving up on this stuff entirely. Please don't. You are exactly where God wants you to be.

A Rediscovery

Looking back on my life, I now realize that God was slowly opening my eyes to rediscover the spiritual growth path He had in mind for me all along. Being somewhat thickheaded, it took me awhile— several years actually. But I'll never forget the day all these puzzle pieces of my past experiences, my drivenness and disillusionment, as well as my understanding of the Bible, began to fall into place in a way that radically impacted my life.

I had asked a pastor friend to join me for lunch because I had a question for him. Over the course of several months, I had noticed that Shane was always talking about the gospel—which I realize is normal for us pastor types—but he would talk about the gospel in a way that was different than I'd ever heard before. I knew all about the gospel, how Jesus had died on the cross for our sins and how through faith in Him we could enter into a relationship with God. I knew all about that and had preached it for years, but there was something in the way Shane talked about the gospel that intrigued me.

As I asked him about this during lunch that day, he explained to me how the gospel is not only for the lost but also for the found. Shane claimed we all need the gospel preached to us every moment of every day, because the gospel is the *means* whereby we experience authentic transformation. Now I'm not intending to sound overly dramatic, but at that moment I honestly felt like a blind man beginning to see. I felt like a little kid at Christmas who, while unwrapping a gift, suddenly realizes what the gift is and can't wait to get it out of the package. I began to see the gospel in a totally different way—in fact, I began to *hear* the gospel in a totally different way.

Not long ago, my wife, Raylene, asked me about a song on a particular CD that I had in my car. Having borrowed my car one day, she happened to listen to this song and had been touched by it. Now I'm one of those people who remembers words to songs very easily, so when she mentioned it, I immediately began reciting the lyrics to her. "But what does the song *mean?*" she asked me. I didn't know. I was familiar with the words but didn't really know what they meant. The next time I was in my car I cued the CD player to that song and settled in to listen. After thirty seconds, I was weeping. I had listened to the song dozens of times and was familiar with the lyrics, but I had never really *heard* the music.

That is exactly how many of us experience the gospel. We understand the content of the gospel—that Jesus died on the cross for our sins. We humbly received this good news at some point in our lives and experienced a genuine conversion. We look for opportunities to share the gospel with others. We are familiar with the lyrics of the gospel … but are not really hearing its music in our soul. Listen to how Rose Marie Miller describes her own experience: *"I love to be in control. I am addicted to duty, order, my rights, my ways, and to outward performance. I am outwardly moral, yet inside I am full of anxieties, fears and guilt. For years, I heard the words of the gospel, but I never heard the music."*[1] Could it be possible that our fears, our addictions, our control issues, and our relational difficulties are not a result of our lack of trying or our lack of sincerity, but rather are due to how clearly we're hearing the gospel's music in our souls?

Good News or Old News

Now I have a hunch some of you are thinking to yourselves, *Oh, the gospel. I already know this. This is basic stuff that I learned a long time ago.* Whenever I tell anyone this book is about living the gospel, there is an immediate and almost universal glaze that settles into his or her eyes. It's the glaze of familiarity. We think we understand the gospel, but the truth is most of us don't. I was a Christian for decades and a senior pastor for years, faithfully preaching the gospel to the lost, but

I now realize I had only scratched the surface in understanding the impact the gospel can have in our everyday lives as Christians. I'm not alone. I believe that most Christ-followers have far too shallow an understanding of the gospel, and because of that, our spiritual lives are not what God intended or what we would want them to be.

So what's our deal with the gospel? It's not that we don't believe it or that we don't desire to share it with others. Our problem is that we aren't necessarily being transformed by it in the present. Why is that? Why aren't we hearing its music? Here's my take on it. For many of us, the good news of the gospel has unintentionally become yesterday's news. We tend to think of the gospel as the *entry point* into Christianity, the wedding music of our spiritual lives. Let me explain.

When Raylene and I got married, we had lots of music in our ceremony—the traditional stuff and some contemporary. I was moved by the music throughout the entire ceremony. But you know what? I don't voluntarily listen to any of that music anymore; in fact, I haven't since our wedding day. It powerfully reflected the beginning of our lives together but not the everyday continuation of our relationship. I believe that the gospel was never intended to solely be the wedding music of our relationship with Jesus, an expression of the *beginning* of our lives with Christ. Rather, it is to be a life-giving song that is heard in our souls every moment of our spiritual lives—a beautiful sound track that plays from beginning to end.

For those of you who aren't really into music, how about another metaphor to describe our experience with the gospel. Many of us tend to view the gospel as the starting line of our lives with Christ. Once the "gospel gun" goes off, we are earnestly running the race, trying our best to grow spiritually. But from a biblical perspective, the gospel is not simply the starting line. It is the race itself. The gospel is *how* spiritual transformation happens.

But Is It Biblical?

Now this all sounds fine and good, but is this what the Bible teaches? Does the New Testament really talk about the gospel in this way? Immediately after my lunch conversation with my friend, I went back to my office to examine this further for myself. I began looking at passages of Scripture that discuss the gospel, passages I had read dozens of times. I turned to Colossians 1 where Paul is writing to *believers* who have already embraced the gospel, and he says to them, "All over the world this gospel is bearing fruit and growing, just as it has been doing among you *since* the day you heard it and understood God's grace in all its truth" (Col. 1:6). He is talking about how the gospel is *continuing* to bear fruit and to grow in the lives of these believers who had already received it.

I turned to the book of Romans, which I believe is the most complete description of the gospel contained in the New Testament. In chapter 1, Paul writes to *believers* in Rome, saying, "That is why I am so eager to preach the gospel also to you who are at Rome" (Rom. 1:15). Now why would Paul need to preach the gospel to people who had already embraced it? He knew what I was just beginning to hear. That we need the gospel preached to us every day, every moment of our lives. In my office that afternoon, I became convinced that Paul understood the gospel in this way, but I also began to wonder … what about Jesus' perspective? Did He understand the gospel in this way as well? Did He preach the gospel as the entry point into Christianity or as a way of life?

I opened my Bible to Matthew 4 and read how Jesus' ministry began: He "was going throughout all Galilee … proclaiming the gospel of the kingdom" (Matt. 4:23 NASB). The gospel of the *kingdom*. It was not simply a gospel of forgiveness, an entryway into God's presence. Jesus was preaching a gospel of continual life transformation, as described immediately after this in the Beatitudes and in the next few verses (Matt. 5:3–16). The language of "kingdom" implies a life constantly influenced and impacted by the King. Jesus was and is inviting us to experience the gospel of the kingdom every moment of every day.

I remember an old Corn Flakes commercial that ended with the phrase "Taste them again for the first time." That's how I suddenly felt about the gospel. It was as if I was tasting it again for the first time, experiencing it in a way that would begin to radically impact my life and the lives of many others around me. Suddenly the gospel was not just about our initial salvation experience but was about our everyday life with Jesus, a continual melody to dance to. I now saw the gospel as a way of life.

But what exactly does that mean? So the gospel is a way of life—but what kind of life? How exactly does the gospel impact our day-to-day experiences—our work, our marriages, our friendships, our activities, our prayer lives, our battles against temptation? What does the gospel have to do with these things? How can this good news radically impact every part of our lives?

Living the Gospel

At the heart of the gospel is the glorious good news that Jesus, God's Son, died voluntarily on the cross, a complete and total sacrifice for our sins (1 Cor. 15:3–4). At that wonderful moment of initially turning to Christ, we hear two distinct melodies of the gospel that together are music to our souls. We hear the melody of *brokenness*—that we are sinners desperately in need of a Savior. And we hear the melody of *faith*—that there is an all-sufficient Savior named Jesus who paid the price we couldn't pay, who lived the life we couldn't live. In Him, we place our trust. At that moment of conversion, these two distinct melodies—brokenness and faith—begin playing in our souls and bringing joy and life. Do you remember your initial experience with Christ when you realized with a heavy heart the depth of your sin and at the same moment the sufficiency of His grace to meet you in that place? That was the music of the gospel. Wasn't it glorious?

But unfortunately, what starts out in our souls as the William Tell Overture slowly becomes elevator Muzak we hardly pay attention to. Very soon after our conversion, the life-giving melodies of brokenness and faith unintentionally get drowned out by a growing and incessant drumbeat that sounds so spiritual: "*Just try harder. Just try harder. Just try harder.*" The cadence of this drumbeat begins to drive our spiritual lives. "You *were* broken, but now you are getting better. If you do these things Christians are supposed to do, you will continue to grow spiritually—becoming more holy, sinning less and less. God will be more and more pleased with you because of how Christlike you are becoming."

Without even realizing it, the melody of brokenness gets replaced by the march of self-effort; the melody of faith gets overtaken by the relentless drumbeat of performance. "*Just try harder. Just try harder.*" We stop hearing the music of the gospel and begin pursuing a spiritual growth path that is actually *removed* from the gospel! The impact of this subtle shift on our spiritual lives is devastating. Listen to Paul's words to a group of believers who without realizing it were doing this very thing:

> I am astonished that you are so quickly deserting the one who called you by the grace of Christ and are turning to a different gospel—which is really no gospel at all.… You foolish Galatians! Who has bewitched you? Before your very eyes Jesus Christ was clearly portrayed as crucified. I would like to learn just one thing from you: Did you receive the Spirit by observing the law, or by believing what you heard? Are you so foolish? *After beginning with the Spirit, are you now trying to attain your goal by human effort?* (Gal. 1:6–7; 3:1–3)

We could summarize Paul's words very succinctly: "What the heck are you doing?" or "How in the world did this happen?" Paul was not mildly concerned. He was beside himself with frustration. What could possibly provoke Paul to such a response? Were these believers renouncing Christ? Were they following other gods? No. What they were doing was politely relegating the gospel to their salvation experience alone and then trying to attain spiritual growth another way—through human effort. *"Just try harder."* They began with the gospel but were now trying to attain their goal apart from the gospel, which will not work.

Gospel Drift

Every one of us is vulnerable to this gospel drift in our spiritual lives. Without realizing it, we stop hearing the melodies of brokenness and faith and instead begin pursuing a spirituality of self-effort and self-sufficiency. We can look and feel so spiritual—and the Enemy of our souls loves it. This was the same way he seduced Adam and Eve in Genesis 3. Not by appealing to their desire for blatant rebellion but rather by tapping into their vulnerability to spiritual self-sufficiency: "For God knows that when you eat of it your eyes will be opened, and you will be like God, knowing good and evil" (Gen. 3:5). Do you hear what Satan whispered to their souls? "Don't trust God on this one. Trust yourself. You'll be better off if you do this on your own." It doesn't sound *that* evil, does it?

This is what makes gospel drift so insidious—we often don't see it. I didn't ... for years. For much of my Christian life I pursued and encouraged others to pursue a spiritual growth path that was removed from the gospel. It looked so spiritual on the outside, but it was ultimately rooted in self—in the fundamental belief that through discipline and effort I was becoming more Christlike. You may be thinking, *Well, isn't that what spiritual growth is all about? Aren't we supposed to be becoming more Christlike?* Certainly, but the critical question is, *how* does that happen? How do we become Christlike?

For most Christians, the goal of Christlikeness is thought to be achieved through certain spiritual activities—prayer, Bible study, giving, church attendance. Now all of these things are good and helpful activities, but do they *make* us more Christlike? Do they *make* us less sinful? That's what I believed for years ... until one day I had a frightening realization: When we define spiritual growth as *us* becoming more like Christ, as *us* becoming less and less sinful, what we are actually pursuing is a spiritual growth path in which we need Jesus less and less. I need Him less today than yesterday, because the power of sin is not as strong in my life. Is that what spiritual maturity looks like?

Gospel Music

In this book, I want to offer a different path to Christlikeness, an alternative approach to spiritual growth. What would happen if instead of subtly turning down the music of the gospel immediately after our conversions, we turned it up? What would happen if the melodies of brokenness and faith were continually and increasingly playing in our souls throughout our spiritual journeys? Here's what would happen: Rather than trying harder to be less and less sinful, we would experience the authentic transformation we long to experience. Don't believe me? Then keep reading … as we together turn up the volume of brokenness and faith in our lives.

For Personal Reflection/Response

- How much of your spiritual experience would you describe as "trying hard"? Is it 10 percent? 50 percent? 75 percent? What is the effect of this in your life—spiritually, emotionally, and physically?

- In this chapter, the gospel was described as a familiar yet "unheard" song. What might happen if you listened to one of your favorite songs in a different way? Give it a try. For example, if you usually listen to a song in your car, try listening to it at home, or print off the lyrics and sit somewhere and sing along. The goal is to listen to a familiar

song, but rather than simply hearing the words, let your
heart experience it. How does the song impact you differently than before?

- As you think about your spiritual life at this moment in
  time, would you say there is a *greater* sense of your need for
  Jesus than a year ago? How do you feel about your answer
  to that question?

✳ ✳ ✳

Heavenly Father, help me understand this
incredible thing called the gospel so that I don't
miss its life-changing melody. I ask You, by the power
of the Holy Spirit, to open my spiritual ears so that
I might hear afresh the melodies of brokenness and faith.
In Jesus' name, amen.

Chapter Two

The Melody of Brokenness

The acknowledgment of our weakness
is the first step in repairing our loss.
—Thomas à Kempis

The greatest of sins is to be conscious of no sin.
—William Barclay

It's not often you see the words *melody* and *brokenness* in the same sentence. As I write this chapter, I am experiencing the pain of a fractured toe. When I stumbled the other day and heard my bone snap, I wasn't really thinking about singing. In my "brokenness" there wasn't a "melody" that seemed to fit—although I could certainly think of some choice lyrics. But from God's perspective, brokenness is an absolutely beautiful melody, enabling us to continually experience the power of the gospel.

Brokenness Defined

What exactly is brokenness? When Jesus began His ministry preaching the gospel of the kingdom, He immediately took some time to describe for His followers exactly what this gospel life entails. In the first few verses of this description (Matt. 5:3–12), Jesus gives us a vivid picture of authentic spirituality—the values His followers are to embrace in order to continually experience the gospel of the kingdom. The first value unveils for us the critical foundation for living this gospel: "Blessed are the poor in spirit, for theirs is the kingdom of heaven" (Matt. 5:3). Blessed are the poor in spirit. Not "blessed are those who have their spiritual act together" or "blessed are the hard workers" or "blessed are the self-sufficient." No. Jesus said, "Blessed are the poor in spirit."

Jesus is not talking about financial poverty but rather a *spiritual* poverty—a desperation of soul in which people, deep in their being, see their spiritual condition before God and realize how completely bankrupt they truly are, utterly powerless in and of themselves. This experience of brokenness is not simply an intellectual acknowledgement but an engagement of the heart. This is why Jesus then says, "Blessed are those who mourn, for they will be comforted" (Matt. 5:4). Jesus is describing a response to being poor in spirit; it causes us to mourn. Rather than being comfortable with our weaknesses and sin, we are saddened by these things in our lives that oppose God's desire. This is what it means to experience the melody of brokenness. It is seeing, really seeing, the depth of our sin from God's perspective.

Now most every Christian would agree this is where the spiritual life *begins*, but that is not what Jesus is saying. A quick read through the rest of these values reveals that these are not onetime events but are to be constantly experienced—mercy, peacemaking, humility, and brokenness. Jesus is inviting us to live every moment in a conscious awareness of how spiritually needy we are, how utterly sinful we are. He invites us to *continually* embrace and experience the melody of brokenness.

Got Thirst?

In addition to the "poor in spirit" description in Matthew 5, there are other vivid images Jesus uses in His teaching to describe the ongoing nature of brokenness. In John 7:37 Jesus declares, "If anyone is thirsty, let him come to me and drink." In that society, drinking water was not even remotely as accessible as it is to us. The thought of someone dying of thirst today is almost inconceivable but not in that culture. A traveler in Jesus' day who found himself without water was in a life-threatening situation. Hopeless. Everyone hearing Jesus' words that day recognized the utter seriousness of being thirsty. It was a life-and-death issue. The psalmist gives us a graphic picture of this condition: "As the deer pants for streams of water, so my soul pants for you, O God" (Ps. 42:1). Deer don't usually pant, unless they are exceedingly frantic for water. So when Jesus is speaking of thirst in John 7, He is not talking about a casual need but rather a desolate, parched soul who will not survive without finding water. To be broken is to be thirsty at any moment in time, realizing how desperately you need Jesus for your spiritual survival.

Jesus uses other vivid language to describe brokenness in Matthew 11:28: "Come to me, all you who are weary and burdened, and

I will give you rest." Here brokenness is equated with being weary of striving, burdened by spiritual to-do lists that never seem to make us any better. In that experience of spiritual brokenness, Jesus invites us to come to Him. These images of brokenness—poverty of spirit, thirst of soul, weariness of self-effort—are all powerful reminders of the critical importance of this to our spiritual lives. Jesus invites us to experience ongoing brokenness, seeing with increasing clarity the depth of our need and realizing our complete inability to live the spiritual life in our own power.

Another word for this brokenness is *repentance*. I know that for many people, the word "repentance" feels a bit negative and even oppressive, bringing to mind images of fiery, pulpit-pounding preachers urging us to stop our sinful behavior or else. Because of these images, we often only think about repentance in response to those really bad sins we occasionally fall into. But from a biblical perspective, repentance is neither oppressive nor occasional. It is a continual experience of seeing our sin the way God does, being confronted with the reality of how broken we really are. The foundation for repentance is not as much about *stopping* our sin as it is about *seeing* it differently. In the story of the prodigal son, Jesus makes it clear exactly what moved the rebellious son to return to his father: "When he came to his senses ..." (Luke 15:17). He *saw* his sin from God's perspective. That seeing is life-changing, which is why it is to be a constant attitude of our hearts.[1] When Martin Luther in AD 1517 nailed his Ninety-five Theses to the church door in Wittenberg, Germany, the first one read: "Our Lord and Master Jesus Christ willed the entire life of believers to be one of repentance." Luther was articulating that the essence of authentic spiritual experience is in seeing—truly seeing—the depth of our brokenness.

How Well Do We See?

Not long ago, my wife and I decided to replace the ten-year-old carpet in our living room. Over the years, we had prided ourselves on how nice the carpet looked despite the intense and constant use it receives from our four children. We had taken great care to vacuum often and diligently remove any stains. Even in our contentment with the carpet's condition, we thought it would be nice to have a different look in that room, so we ordered new carpet. As we were preparing the room for the installers, we began to tear out this wonderful carpet and discovered to our horror that it was anything but wonderful. We gazed upon pet stains we had been blissfully unaware of and various other discolorations from who knows what or when. As if that wasn't bad enough, the pad underneath the carpet had enough dust and dirt to plant a garden—it wasn't quite that bad, but you get the point. Suddenly the thought of sitting on that carpet, or lying down on that carpet, or wrestling with kids on that carpet—all of which we had done many times—made my stomach turn. It was amazing the difference that resulted when we actually began seeing the truth.

Let me suggest that this is the way we all tend to live our spiritual lives. Rather than really seeing the truth about our spiritual condition before God, we tend to assume we're doing pretty well. After all, we do the vacuuming of confession fairly often, and when we're aware of a stain, we immediately respond. But what's underneath all that? What's really going on below the decent-looking surface of our lives? Quite honestly, we'd rather not go there, if at all possible. It's a bit of the "ignorance is bliss" perspective. The less we know the better. However, what we don't realize is that the spiritual implications of this perspective are huge.

Jesus once said "Then you will know the truth, and the truth will set you free" (John 8:32). While we may prefer at times to be ignorant of the truth about ourselves, that indifference will inevitably lead us away from the freedom of living the gospel. Imagine having a life-threatening cancer rapidly growing in your body. While that is certainly a horrible situation, there is actually something far worse: not *knowing* you have a cancer growing in your body. If you don't know you're sick, you won't go to a doctor for help. Ignorance about a disease is of no benefit to the person with the disease. No wonder Jesus said, "It is not the healthy who need a doctor, but the sick" (Matt. 9:12). The life-giving melody of the gospel is released most fully in those who admit how desperately they need it. If we don't see the depth of our need, we won't rely on Jesus for help.

In order to more deeply hear the melody of brokenness, you must continually see a very life-giving and yet unsettling spiritual reality: *You are a lot more sinful than you realize.* The gospel, when rightly understood, forces us to constantly face the truth about ourselves—that sin deeply penetrates our beings. Many Christians think the bulk of our sin problem was taken care of at our conversions. After all, at that moment our sin was forgiven—past, present, and future. We now struggle at times with doing sinful things but not like we used to before we received Christ. But is that true? Has our propensity to sin truly decreased? It all depends on how deeply you look.

Sin Redefined

If I asked you to define *sin*, what would you say? Nearly all Christians define sin as "doing bad things." You know the list:

> Don't lie.
> Don't steal.
> Don't lust.
> Don't be greedy.

If avoiding these behaviors is our standard, then most of us will feel okay about ourselves. We know we are not perfect, but by and large, we are doing pretty well. We mess up a few times a day, but that's not too bad. But from God's perspective, sin is much more than simply "doing bad things." *Sin is the deeply rooted tendency in all of us to live with self as the center of our lives rather than God.* Jesus gave us a very clear standard, to which anything short of is sin: "Love the Lord your God with all your heart and with all your soul and with all your mind and with all your strength" (Mark 12:30). Anytime we love anything—including ourselves—more than God, that's sin. John Stott writes, "The essence of sin is man substituting himself for God."[2] Sin goes way beyond just doing something bad. It is the unyielding and tenacious desire in us to want to be the center of the universe. We want to be noticed, to be affirmed, to be valued, to be worshipped, to be in control, to be comfortable, to be successful. These are not just casual interests—very often they drive our lives.

When we define sin in this way, we suddenly realize that it is no small problem. It permeates our entire beings, influencing every action as it infiltrates our very attitudes and motivations. I remember hearing Larry Crabb once say "A husband kissing his wife could be sinful." Now you may be thinking, *Come on … how could something as loving and good as a husband kissing his wife be sinful?* It all depends upon the motive of the husband's heart. Is he kissing his wife as an expression of love for her, or is he kissing her in order to receive something from her in return? Sin is not just doing bad things but also includes doing good things from a self-centered motivation.

One Sunday afternoon, I was reflecting upon that morning's worship services at our church and felt really good about the message I had given. The hard work had paid off as several people had mentioned to me after the service how helpful it was to them. But my encouragement about the services was also mixed with disappointment because the attendance was much smaller than I had hoped. I began to be bothered because several key people in our church were not there to hear my "powerful" message. I started to feel a bit angry—"righteous" anger of course!—that these people had not come to church. They needed to hear this.

In the midst of my growing frustration with these absent people, I sensed the Lord gently asking me a question: "Alan, what is all this frustration really about? Is this truly about Me and My purposes in their lives, or is it about you and your desire for people to be impressed with your sermon and to appreciate *your* hard work?" Ouch. I suddenly realized the frustration I had attributed to spiritual maturity on my part was actually rooted in my own pride and self-centeredness. Having these people in church met some need in me for affirmation. Yuck … and it got worse. I began to see how my whole ministry passion—to grow a larger church—was a passion entrenched as deeply in my ego as it was in Christ's glory. Maybe more.

I was laid bare before God as I saw the revolting depth of my self-absorption and pride. It was painful to look at and even more painful to admit to God, but in that moment of seeing, I offered to Him a heartfelt prayer of confession. On that Sunday afternoon, I was hearing more clearly the melody of brokenness as I saw how acutely I needed a gospel that could deal with more than my "doing bad things." I needed a gospel that could meet me in the pervasive sinfulness that penetrated my everyday life.

The Iceberg

I remember seeing a captivating image of an iceberg, fascinating because it revealed the iceberg from both above and below the waterline. The portion above the waterline was a relatively small, jagged section of ice. But below the waterline, it was absolutely enormous. I later found out that, according to scientific research, seven-eighths of an iceberg lies below the water. When I think about the reality of sin in all of our lives, that photograph often comes to mind. The sins we are consciously aware of, those that are above the waterline, seem relatively small—a few misbehaviors here and there. But using God's definition of sin reveals there is a lot below the waterline of which we are unaware.

For many sincere Christians, spiritual maturity is about trying hard to decrease the size of the iceberg above the waterline. With a few sermons and some behavioral adjustments, we can manage to do just that. The end result is a superficial spirituality that will never change our lives much. God's heart is that we would increasingly see below the waterline, so that we would continually realize how desperately we need a Savior.

The Tongue as a Tool

Your deepening experience of living the gospel is directly related to your ability or willingness to truly see the depth of your sin. Do you realize how desperately you need a Savior every moment of every day? Do you really see the depth of your self-centeredness and self-worship? Here's a little experiment I would encourage you to try. It's called the Tongue Assignment.[3]

For one week, do not …

- Gossip (or spread a bad report)
- Complain
- Criticize
- Boast
- Blame shift
- Defend yourself
- Deceive others

Try it for a week. How long could you go without doing any of these things? A week? A day? An hour? Five minutes? When a friend of mine heard me give this "Tongue Assignment" in a sermon, he was convinced he could do it for a week and committed himself to do so. Moments later as someone's cell phone rang in the worship service, he instinctively turned to his wife to complain about this person's rudeness and was struck with a realization: He couldn't even make it through the message without complaining! Jesus made it very clear that our words are a window into our inner beings. "For out of the overflow of the heart the mouth speaks.… For out of the heart come evil thoughts, murder, adultery, sexual immorality, theft, false testimony, slander" (Matt. 12:34; 15:19). What do your words reveal about the prevalence of self in your life?

I'll never forget my first speeding ticket. My instinctive response was to blame someone else ("I thought she told me the speed limit in this state is seventy-five miles per hour"), then justify my actions ("I didn't see any speed limit signs"), and finally resort to criticizing ("Doesn't that policeman have anything better to do with his time?"). Rather than humbly accepting responsibility, my words revealed a commitment to self at all costs. And that is just one area of my life! What about every other way in which self-centeredness influences my actions, my motives, or my thoughts? Our problem is not so much the *presence* of sin but the fact that we don't see it. A crucial part of God's heart is to help us see the depth of our need, to hear the melody of brokenness—but it is a hard melody to hear.

A Spiritual Setup?

In the first part of the book of Romans, Paul does a masterful job helping us hear the melody of our brokenness, and he does it in such a subversive way that we don't realize it until it happens. Immediately after introducing the gospel in Romans 1:17 (which we will look at in detail in chapter 5), Paul launches into a detailed description of the damage and destruction happening in our world because of sinful behavior. It starts with thanklessness and unbelief, which lead to lust, then transitions to more perverted lusts, and eventually to rage and abuse.

> They have become filled with every kind of wicked-
> ness, evil, greed and depravity. They are full of envy,

murder, strife, deceit and malice. They are gossips,
slanderers, God-haters, insolent, arrogant and boast-
ful; they invent ways of doing evil; they disobey their
parents; they are senseless, faithless, heartless, ruthless. Although they know God's righteous decree that
those who do such things deserve death, they not only
continue to do these very things but also approve of
those who practice them. (Rom. 1:29–32)

Notice the third-person pronoun. *They* do this. *They* do that. You
can almost feel the church at Rome hearing these words and rising up
in indignation and us rising up with them—yes, our world is sinful
and bad. Those people out there are so evil. They hate God and are
proud and ruthless. How horrible it is to live in this world with those
evil people out there—the murderers and terrorists and adulterers. Do
you feel it? How often has Romans 1 been quoted to talk about the
evils of our sinful world and our separation from all that?

Look carefully at what Paul says in the very next verse: "You,
therefore, have no excuse, you who pass judgment on someone else,
for at whatever point you judge the other, you are condemning yourself, because you who pass judgment do the same things" (Rom. 2:1).
Did you notice the pronoun is no longer *they* but *you*? He is writing
to Christians, and he says, "You who pass judgment do the same
things." He is exposing our self-righteous attitudes—how easily we
look down upon the sins of others without taking an honest look at
ourselves. An honest look at ourselves?

Okay, let's try that for a moment. Question: There's a photograph
of a group of people, and you're one of the people. You pick up the

picture, and whom do you look for first … maybe even second and third? That's right—yourself. Which of us is not a lover of self? If I look a bit more deeply, I realize that I spent most of my day thinking about myself. I was focused on accomplishing *my* agenda—no interruptions, please. In conversations I was intent on offering *my* perspective, thinking to myself, *Please hurry up and finish what you are saying so I can share what I want to say.* I felt jealous and angry when hearing a friend rave about another pastor's speaking ability. I freely criticized people, then realized to my horror they were standing outside my office. In response, I worried more about what they now thought of me than about how their hearts felt. I spent a few minutes grumbling about a certain situation, then went back to preparing a sermon in which I specifically addressed the issue of grumbling. I haven't even mentioned the defensiveness, the impatience, the drivenness, the greed, the lust that at various times pulled at my heart today.

Folks, this is me. And this is us. Sin is not just a little inconvenience we struggle with periodically, a minor thing in our lives. Sin permeates our beings. Our motives are self-centered. Our agendas are self-driven. Our lives are self-absorbed. *We are a lot more sinful than we ever realized.* The truth is: We are broken. Years ago, a *London Times* editorial ended with the question "What's wrong with the world?" G. K. Chesterton, a well-known philosopher and theologian, chose to reply with this response:

> Dear Editor:
>   What's wrong with the world? I am.
>   Faithfully yours,
>   G. K. Chesterton[4]

New Creation?

Now some of you are thinking, *Hold it. So what then did Christ do when I became a Christian? I thought I was a new creation.* You are! The moment you say yes to Jesus, you are spiritually reborn. Your spirit (i.e., your inner being) is washed, redeemed, made alive. You are given a new heart (Ezek. 11:19), and in that heart the very presence of Christ comes to live forever (Rom. 8:9–10; Col. 1:27). At the core of your being you are a new person. That is all wonderfully true. But there is another reality at work in our bodies. It's what the Bible refers to as our "flesh" or our "sinful nature"—that part of us that is still utterly self-absorbed. The presence of this reality makes for an interesting dynamic in our spiritual lives.

In fact, listen to Paul's description of his spiritual experience after becoming a Christian. "I know that nothing good lives in me, that is, in my sinful nature. For I have the desire to do what is good, but I cannot carry it out" (Rom. 7:18). Notice the personal battle Paul is describing. In his inner being, he has "the desire to do what is good." That desire is evidence of the new heart he has been given at conversion. But that desire is significantly influenced by the flesh—this overpowering pull toward rebellion against God. It is an incredibly frustrating struggle, which Paul goes on to describe in further detail:

> For what I do is not the good I want to do; no, the
> evil I do not want to do—this I keep on doing.
> Now if I do what I do not want to do, it is no longer
> I who do it, but it is sin living in me that does it. So
> I find this law at work: When I want to do good,
> evil is right there with me. For in my inner being, I

delight in God's law; but I see another law at work in the members of my body, waging war against the law of my mind and making me a prisoner of the law of sin at work within my members. (Rom. 7:19–23)

Notice, Paul is not saying that we are spiritual worms, incapable of good. He freely acknowledges that in the deepest part of our beings (i.e., our hearts), we long for God's will. But Paul also is painfully aware that there is another very real and powerful force at work in our bodies, constantly pulling us toward self-absorption and self-centeredness. This is our reality. Sin is not a simply a minor struggle. It is a very real part of our lives as Christians.

Good News, Please

Wow, Alan. Thanks so much for really encouraging me in my Christian walk. I know, I know. The thought of admitting the depth of our sinfulness and embracing this melody of brokenness doesn't sound very helpful at all. Please stay with me here. The melody of brokenness is an incredibly beautiful melody because of what happens in our souls *in the midst* of our brokenness. When Paul saw the depth of his need in Romans 7, he was freed to look beyond himself for help: "What a wretched man I am! Who will rescue me from this body of death? Thanks be to God—through Jesus Christ our Lord!" (Rom. 7:24–25). Hearing the melody of brokenness enabled Paul to also hear the melody of faith, discovering his need of a Savior who was more sufficient than he ever dreamed. This is what brokenness does in our lives. This is why to be poor in spirit is the foundation for vibrant spirituality. To realize our brokenness is to open the door to experiencing Jesus more fully.

Now one might say, "But hold it, Alan. I thought this passage in Romans 7 was not a reflection of Paul's entire life but rather an immature period early in his spiritual life. Surely Paul grew out of this so that this battle with sin was less and less intense." Listen to what Paul says in a letter written near the end of his life: "Here is a trustworthy saying that deserves full acceptance: Christ Jesus came into the world to save sinners—of whom I am the worst" (1 Tim. 1:15). Notice, Paul does not say, "I *was* the worst of sinners but am no longer that bad." No. Paul says, "I *am* the worst of sinners." Present tense. Over the course of his life, Paul had a growing awareness of his sinfulness, a growing conviction that he was far more sinful than he ever realized. This deepening awareness of his brokenness enabled him to more fully experience the sufficiency of Christ. It was this reality that would move Paul to declare:

> Therefore I will boast all the more gladly about my weaknesses, so that Christ's power may rest on me. That is why, for Christ's sake, I delight in weaknesses, in insults, in hardships, in persecutions, in difficulties. For when I am weak, then I am strong. (2 Cor. 12:9–10)

When I am weak, then I am strong. That's what makes brokenness so powerful and beneficial in our lives. It can lead us to a deepening dependence upon the sufficiency of Christ (which is what the second half of this book is about).

How deeply do you see your sinfulness? How aware are you of the ways in which self-centeredness influences your life and drives your behavior? Until you begin to see the depth of your sinfulness, you can never truly understand the power and wonder of the gospel. So rejoice! You are a far worse sinner than you realize!

For Personal Reflection/Response

- Is the thought of more clearly hearing the melody of brokenness freeing or frightening? Why do you think that is? (You may want to ask the Lord to show you why.)

- How accurately does the phrase "poor in spirit" describe your experience with Christ right now?

- Try the Tongue Assignment (on page 46) for a day or two. What was that experience like for you? What did you see about yourself that you hadn't seen before?

✳ ✳ ✳

Heavenly Father, I need Your help to see more deeply
the reality of my own sinfulness and self-centeredness.
I confess, I so often live as though I want to be God.
I want the glory. I want to be in control. I want to be
noticed and valued. I am far more sinful than I ever
realized. Holy Spirit, help me to continually live in the
freedom of being poor in spirit. Help me to recognize more
and more the depth of my thirst for You. Help me to hear
more clearly and continuously the melody of brokenness.
In Jesus' name, amen.

Chapter Three

If It's Broken, Fix It!

Before you can be certain that Jesus Christ is in your heart,
you must be brought to see not only that your sins must
be done away with but also your righteousness.
—*George Whitefield*

I'm not much of a handyman. I warned my wife before we were married that it's just not something I do. If duct tape won't fix it, I'm calling in reinforcements. However, I do remember a moment fairly early in our marriage when Raylene asked me to fix a clogged drain. So I got out all our books on do-it-yourself home repairs—books my wife had purchased, not me—and started unscrewing pipes. Before I knew it, the problem was solved. With wrench in hand I did a victory dance around the house while humming the theme song from *Rocky*.

When we encounter something in our lives that is broken—our computer, our car, our phone, our golf swing—it is our instinctive response to fix it or to call someone who can. We like to fix things that are broken. So when we hear, as the last chapter asserted, that we are broken and far more sinful than we realize, our instinctive human and even Christian response is to try to fix it ourselves. After all, we don't like being broken. We don't like feeling needy. We are motivated to do something about it, but what are we to do? It's here that many of us make a serious mistake: We try to be good. We try to be better Christians.

The Danger of Being Good

The Bible introduces us to a group of sincere, devout people whose primary objective in life was to be good. In their passionate desire to please God, they committed themselves to earnestly seeking how to best follow God's commands. They were people of prayer, giving, and devotion to God's Word. Models of spiritual maturity, they set an example for others to follow in their zeal to obey God. Jesus often interacted with these folks, otherwise known as the Pharisees, and had some very choice words to describe their approach to the spiritual life:

> Woe to you, teachers of the law and Pharisees, you hypocrites! You clean the outside of the cup and dish, but inside they are full of greed and self-indulgence. Blind Pharisee! First clean the inside of the cup and dish, and then the outside also will be clean. (Matt. 23:25–26)

Not exactly a ringing endorsement. And this is not the only place Jesus issues such a strong rebuke toward the Pharisees. It is a constant theme in His ministry. Jesus' strongest denunciations were directed not toward the immoral and corrupt but rather toward moral people who sincerely wanted to do what was right. (Better read that last sentence again because it's really important and easily missed.) *Trying* to be good doesn't get us any closer to God. In fact, it tends to move us in the opposite direction—away from living the gospel. What's up here? What could possibly be wrong with a sincere Christian trying hard to be good?

Several years ago a friend of mine and I decided to hold each other accountable in regard to an area of sin with which we both struggled: sexual lust. After awhile we realized our accountability really had no "sting" in it if one of us fell into this sin. There was no real negative consequence, so we decided to up the ante a bit: twenty dollars given to the other person for every sinful lapse. It worked for several weeks as neither of gave in to lustful thoughts. Surely a definitive spiritual victory, right? We certainly avoided the top sin on our list … or did we?

In the midst of our battle for purity, I came to a troubling realization: The main reason we were avoiding lust was because of our greed—neither of us wanted to lose twenty bucks! Our one deadly sin had simply been overtaken by another. We were trying to be good, but in reality we were treating a spiritual cancer with a Band-Aid. Our external obedience in avoiding one sin had blinded us to our real problem—the sin beneath the sin. A pastor friend of mine often says, "The sin beneath every sin is our desire to be God." In our struggle to overcome lust, neither of us took the time to look more deeply at the root cause of this lust—the craving to be worshipped and affirmed, the attempt to find life in more of self. Even though we had avoided the external behavior, all this other stuff was still very much alive and well in us, feeding our lust and our greed. Ultimately, our attempt at being good fostered a superficial holiness and blinded us to the depth of our idolatry.

Not only that, I also began to notice during those weeks of "purity" how my definition of lust had an ever-expanding loophole. A lingering gaze at a bikini-clad supermodel on TV didn't really count nor did a brief perusal through a Victoria's Secret catalog. That twenty bucks was for *real* lust. Without even realizing it, my best efforts at being good were actually removing me from living the gospel. I was priding myself for following my list of holy behaviors and yet all the while ignoring the depth of my own sinfulness.

The Good, the Bad, and the Accepted

Trying to be good will never fix our brokenness. In fact, it often compounds the problem. Jesus once gave a vivid picture of this by describing two men who went to the temple to pray. One man was a very devout Pharisee, a well-respected religious leader in the community. The other man was a tax collector, a profession highly despised by the culture since tax collectors were notorious for corruption and greed.

> The Pharisee stood up and prayed about himself: "God, I thank you that I am not like other men—robbers, evildoers, adulterers—or even like this tax collector. I fast twice a week and give a tenth of all I get." But the tax collector stood at a distance. He would not even look up to heaven, but beat his breast and said, "God, have mercy on me, a sinner."

> I tell you that this man, rather than the other, went
> home justified before God. (Luke 18:11–14)

Jesus' conclusion must have absolutely stunned his hearers. Actually "stunned" is a bit of an understatement. Perhaps blown away—totally shocked—beside themselves might describe this better. I mean, imagine the impact if we substituted "beloved senior pastor" and "shady used-car salesman" into the story … you get the idea. Jesus shocks everyone by using the word "justified" to describe the spiritual condition of the tax collector. To be justified means to be made right in the eyes of God, to be completely accepted by Him. Jesus is actually saying the *immoral* tax collector goes home in right standing with God while the *moral* religious leader doesn't! How can that be? The answer is simple: Even though both men were broken— desperately sinful and needy—only one of them was willing to admit it, to call himself a sinner. The tax collector heard the melody of brokenness and cried out to God for mercy. In his spiritual poverty, he experienced the complete acceptance and love of God.

The religious leader, on the other hand, refused to hear the melody of brokenness and instead chose a very different response. He chose to try to "fix" his brokenness by asserting his own goodness. "Look at all I have done, Lord. I tithe. I fast. I'm not like this sinner here." Luke describes this Pharisee as being someone who was "confident of his own righteousness" (Luke 18:9). In other words, this person felt closer to God because of his own ability to keep his list of good behaviors. His goodness was getting in the way of the gospel.

We're all vulnerable to this instinctive response—that we can somehow make ourselves more acceptable to God by doing good things. We definitely *feel* more acceptable to God when we are able to keep our list of good behaviors—which is a very dangerous place to be, spiritually speaking. While our list-driven spirituality can look quite "mature" on the outside, it is a path that is filled with spiritual land mines.

Spiritual Blindness 101

One of the dangers of trying to be good is that it blinds us to the depth of our sinfulness. My previously mentioned "victory" over lust blinded me to the depth of my greed. As long as we are keeping *our* list, we feel holy. But how complete is our list? Who comes up with the list, anyway? What sins have we conveniently left off our list? Can we add to the list, take away from the list? What if my list is different from your list?

In the story Jesus told, the Pharisee felt good about himself for diligently keeping his list of good behaviors: giving, fasting, faithfulness to his spouse, honesty in his business dealings—all of which are very important things to God. But why wasn't the sin of pride on his list or the sin of having a critical spirit toward others? Even though the Pharisee was no doubt familiar with the numerous Old Testament warnings against the danger of spiritual pride (e.g., Prov. 8:13) and the importance of extending mercy (e.g., Hos. 6:6), he conveniently ignored them, thinking instead of how well he had followed *his* list of holy behaviors.

Having been a pastor for a number of years, I have had opportunity to hear numerous sins confessed to me in the privacy of my office: adultery, drug addiction, deception, homosexuality, and pornography, to name a few. I've never had anyone make an appointment to confess to me his or her materialism or prejudice or pride. Those are sins in which most of us regularly participate, and yet they are rarely on our spiritual radar.

Jesus continually exposed the danger of a list-keeping approach to spirituality. In Matthew 5:21–22, Jesus said, "You have heard that it was said to the people long ago, 'Do not murder.' … But I tell you that anyone who is angry with his brother will be subject to judgment." Jesus is pointing out how easily we can keep a list of things to avoid—"I haven't murdered anyone"—and so we feel good about ourselves before God. But the truth is, while we haven't killed anyone physically, we have destroyed people through gossip. We have hated people who have hurt us, continuing to hang on to our bitterness and unforgiveness. So, yes, we are keeping the "do not murder" part of the law but are missing the heart of the command—what a friend of mine refers to as getting the course before the heart.

It's no wonder Jesus got so ticked off with the Pharisees. Their goodness actually blinded them from spiritual reality! Over and over He accused them of this: "Blind Pharisee!" (Matt. 23:26), "Blind fools!" (Matt. 23:17), "Blind guides!" (Matt. 23:24). They couldn't see, and they didn't *know* they couldn't see. Sort of like the newly married man who, after years of independently choosing his own clothing, hears from his bride that infamous question: "You're going to wear *that* to work?" He'd blissfully worn it for years, never knowing it looked awful—until confronted with his own color blindness. Infinitely more dangerous than color blindness is spiritual blindness—not seeing the depth of our sin, not seeing how desperately we need help.

What this ultimately means is that trying to be good can actually keep us further from God than sin ever will. (You may need to read that again!) The most immoral sinner is just one step from acceptance by God, right? The tax collector repented and was immediately accepted by God. But the "good" person who has diligently kept his list is further removed from experiencing God's acceptance, because he doesn't even realize he has a sin problem. By hiding ourselves in our good behaviors, we remove ourselves from the impact of fully experiencing the gospel.

The View of Others

Trying to be good not only distorts our vision of ourselves but also damages our view of others. The Pharisee in Jesus' story not only had an overexaggerated view of himself, but he also looked down on everyone else who didn't meet his "goodness" standard—who didn't keep *his* list. "God, I thank you that I am not like other men— robbers, evildoers, adulterers—or even like this tax collector. I fast twice a week and give a tenth of all I get" (Luke 18:11–12). Can you believe the arrogance of this guy? Thankfully, *we* don't struggle with this … or do we?

Comedian George Carlin once observed, "Have you ever noticed that anybody going slower than you is an idiot and anyone going faster than you is a maniac?"[1] Isn't it interesting how *our* behavior instinctively becomes the standard through which we evaluate others? One morning after a worship service, a man in our church came up to me and asked, "Is it okay for me to have a 'Homosexuality is an abomination to God' bumper sticker on my car?" I responded, "I guess … as long as you also have bumper stickers saying that pride, materialism, and lust are also abominations to God." I haven't seen him in church since that conversation. For many Christians, homosexuality becomes an easy target, but do we really think our attempts to find life in shopping sprees, or business success, or athletic trophies, or plastic surgery, or the approval of others are any less sinful in the eyes of God?

When we are earnestly trying to keep our list of good behaviors, we inevitably become quite critical and judgmental of others who aren't following our list nearly as well as we are. We have our top five "evil behavior" list and make a big deal about those who participate in such practices. Through bumper stickers, T-shirts, letters to the editor, boycotts, or relational distance, we clearly communicate our disdain for those who engage in such things—all the while conveniently oblivious to certain other evil behaviors in our own lives that God also has decidedly strong feelings about: prejudice, a lack of compassion for the poor, materialism, to name a few. It's no wonder the church has such a credibility problem in America—the world sees right through our hypocrisy. It's spiritual blindness. The world can see it in us, but we have a hard time seeing it in ourselves.

Just Give Me a List!

So if diligently keeping a list of good behaviors is such a spiritually destructive thing, why are we as Christians so prone to this? Believe it or not, that question gets answered in the first few pages of the Bible. When Adam and Eve sinned against God in the garden of Eden and were presented with an opportunity to meet with God, how did they respond? "They hid from the LORD God" (Gen. 3:8). Rather than facing the truth about their brokenness, they were ashamed. So they hid—and we've been hiding ever since. Often, we as humans hide through continuing in our sinful rebellion. We run from God and do our own thing.

But there is another way to hide from our shame—by trying to be good. If we can keep a list of good behaviors, we no longer feel ashamed before God. "Look what we've done." There is something within all of us that truly believes we can earn God's favor with our good behaviors. Unfortunately this something doesn't die when we become Christians. In fact, it pulls at us with just as much force as ever before. Although we know we are saved by grace, a part of us still believes that by doing good things, God will like us more. We believe we can fix our brokenness. "Just give me a list, and I'll take care of it!"

Late one evening, I received a phone call from a distraught husband whose wife had just left him. Heartbroken, he assured me of his desire to do anything to get her back. He was desperate. So we began to talk. As I listened to him share his perspective, I suggested that he take some time to look deeply at his own heart and accept responsibility for the hurt he had caused in the relationship. That suggestion was met with silence. After a few minutes of further conversation, I mentioned it again … only to receive the same disinterested response. It was becoming evident that what he wanted was a short list of things to do to get her back—maybe a book to read or a communication technique. It was just as evident what he didn't want—having to look honestly at his heart and his actions. He didn't want to look at his own brokenness, to face the hurt and pain his self-centeredness had caused. He wanted a quick fix, a list of things to do.

Let's be honest. Lists are a whole lot easier than looking honestly at our own brokenness. So many Christian books and so much of

Christian teaching today have this as the basic theme: "Here's what pleases God. Go do it." We long for five steps, four habits, six principles … any list of behaviors that can help make our lives work better. Please hear me: I'm not questioning our sincerity or our desire. I'm just afraid we're missing the gospel in the midst of this. Trying to be good is, as Jesus once vividly described it, like being "whitewashed tombs" (Matt. 23:27): looking so spiritual on the outside but being filled with the rot of death within. As if that wasn't clear enough, Jesus also told these professional list keepers, "You travel over land and sea to win a single convert, and when he becomes one, you make him twice as much a son of hell as you are" (Matt. 23:15). Apparently the road to hell actually *is* paved with good intentions—even good behaviors. Trying to be good is the absolute antithesis of living the gospel. Why? Because we cannot fix ourselves no matter how hard we try. The continual reality of the gospel is that we are broken, and we can't do a thing to fix it. Trying hard to be good will never result in real transformation. All it does is drown out the music of the gospel.

No Dancing at This Party

Are you familiar with the story of the prodigal son Jesus told in Luke 15? Most of the time, we focus on the lost son who squandered his father's inheritance and in his misery returned to confess his sin, only to be welcomed with open arms by his father. It was time to party! But not everyone attended this celebration of grace.

> Meanwhile, the older son was in the field. When he
> came near the house, he heard music and dancing.

So he called one of the servants and asked him what was going on. "Your brother has come," he replied, "and your father has killed the fattened calf because he has him back safe and sound." The older brother became angry and refused to go in. So his father went out and pleaded with him. But he answered his father, "Look! All these years I've been slaving for you and never disobeyed your orders. Yet you never gave me even a young goat so I could celebrate with my friends. But when this son of yours who has squandered your property with prostitutes comes home, you kill the fattened calf for him!" (Luke 15:25–30)

Not everyone is celebrating. When the older brother "heard music and dancing," he became angry. He certainly wasn't going to be dancing at *this* party. Why did the music of grace result in such an angry response? He explains his reasons. "C'mon, Dad. For years I've been slaving for you and done everything you asked. But you never even let me have a party with my friends!" Do you hear the drumbeat of performance? He had tried so hard to be good. He had been the obedient son, doing everything the father wanted him to do. He was the good son, the moral one who kept the rules. But notice his motivation: "All these years I've been slaving for you" (v. 29). His motivation to be good was rooted in duty rather than desire. Here he was, a beloved son, and yet living like he was an employee. Ironically, his "goodness" resulted in his missing the love of his father. To him, his father was a slave driver who was never satisfied—which wasn't true, but that was his perception. Why? Because he was trying to earn the love that was already his, and it distorted his image of his dad. It drowned out the music of the gospel.

In reflection upon this passage, Henri Nouwen honestly admits, "I know, from my own life, how diligently I have tried to be good, acceptable, likable, and a worthy example for others. There was always the conscious effort to avoid the pitfalls of sin and the constant fear of giving in to temptation. But with all of that there came a seriousness, a moralistic intensity … that made it increasingly difficult to feel at home in my Father's house."[2] What a powerful description. Our diligent attempts to be good can make it difficult for us to feel at home in our Father's house, at rest in His incredible love. Nouwen adds, "I became less free, less spontaneous, less playful."[3]

Not long ago, my family attended a wedding reception that culminated in an opportunity for dancing. My six-year-old son immediately seized the moment, rushing to the dance floor the minute the music started, shaking and moving with all his heart. As I looked around at the vast majority of us not on the dance floor, many of whom I think wanted to dance but stayed seated out of concern for our own image or proper protocol, I couldn't help but wonder: When did this happen? When did the spontaneity and selfless abandon we naturally had as children get squeezed out by the debilitating taskmaster of self-consciousness and duty? We could ask the same thing in our spiritual lives. When did the spontaneous joy of celebrating the Father's love for us get replaced by the taskmaster of self-absorption and self-reliance? When was the melody of the Father's love song drowned out by the incessant drumbeat of performance?

In the story of the prodigal son, we see the inevitable result of this shift in focus—not only does desire now feel like duty and the father's love like the expectations of an employer; we also see the joy of contentment becomes the sting of resentment. "Look at all I've done for You, God. Look at how I've obeyed You, and this is how You treat me? All these bad things happen in my life. Don't I deserve better than this?" When we are focused on list keeping and trying to be good, it will inevitably lead to a vending-machine approach to God: I put in my money; out comes what I deserve. And if nothing comes out after I've done my part, I'm pretty mad about it—which is just like the elder brother in the parable. There is a self-righteous anger that is boiling just below the surface of his life, and ironically it's fed by his own obedience.

I love the way the father responds to his son's self-righteous indignation: "'My son,' the father said, 'You are always with me, and everything I have is yours'" (Luke 15:31). Could I paraphrase that? "Son, you don't need to play this 'I obey you in order to earn my way' game any longer. It's not that kind of relationship. My love for you is never to be dependent upon how good you are or how well you perform. Until you see it that way, you will never know the joy of just being my son." For how many of us are our diligent efforts at being *good* actually hindering our experience of being *loved?*

The irony of this "parable of the lost son" is there are actually two lost sons in this story. One is lost in his sinfulness and rebellion, the other in his goodness. The *rebellious* son hears the melody of brokenness and experiences the incredible grace of his loving father. He was lost but now is found. The *obedient* son, however, remains lost in his goodness, separated from his father as he earnestly tries so hard to earn what is already his.

Every moment of our lives, you and I have a choice—to dance to the music of the gospel that meets us in our brokenness and sinfulness or to earnestly attempt to fix our brokenness by trying to be good. As we will see, that choice can make all the difference.

For Personal Reflection/Response

Before going on to the next chapter, I encourage you to stop and prayerfully think about this question: Which "son" do you more often tend to be? Are you usually on the dance floor of the party celebrating the grace of God toward you, or are you on the outside looking in, trusting in your own effort to earn God's love?

Perhaps these questions can help you explore this more deeply:

- When you do good things, do you feel that God loves you more? Or should love you more?

- What are the top sins on your "these don't please God" list? What "lesser" sins have been omitted?

- Do you often find yourself angry at others who don't keep your list?

- Is your spiritual life characterized more by desire or duty? Joy or obligation?

- In your heart of hearts, do you experience God more as a Father to be loved or a Master to be obeyed?

✳ ✳ ✳

Heavenly Father, I confess to You my instinct to
fix my brokenness by trying harder to be good.
My list-keeping tendencies so often keep me from seeing
the depth of my own sin and at the same time encourage
me to be critical of others who aren't keeping my list.
Not only that, my attempts at being good are so often
rooted in a distorted view of who You are. Rather than
celebrating Your grace, I end up trying to earn Your
acceptance through my performance. Help me to more
deeply experience the gospel. In Jesus' name, amen.

Chapter Four

Learning to Hear

Our depressions, jealousies, narcissism, and failures are not at
odds with the spiritual life. Indeed, they are essential to it.
When tended, they prevent the spirit from zooming off
into the ozone of perfectionism and pride.
— Thomas Moore

The fact that the Scriptures are brim full of hustlers, murderers,
cowards, adulterers, and mercenaries used to shock me.
Now it is a source of great comfort.
— Bono

When I was in college, many students who were looking for an easy elective would sign up for a class called Music Listening Lab. It was reputed to be one of the easiest three hours of credit at the university. While I was struggling to stay afloat in my extremely demanding chemical engineering classes, some of my friends were "hard at work" listening to music (not that I'm bitter about it). What no doubt made Music Listening Lab such an easy course was the fact that there was virtually no homework. The goal of the class was not to fill students' minds with book knowledge about music but rather to help them learn how to really *listen* to music—how to discern different types of music and different instrumentation. The only way to learn that was in a laboratory setting where real listening could actually be experienced.

Living the gospel is a lot like that. In order to continually experience the life-giving power of the gospel, we need to learn how to listen to the melody of brokenness in our everyday lives. So how do we do that? How can we better tune in to this life-transforming melody so that we can more fully embrace our Savior? Well, I've got good news and bad news. The bad news is, we can't. While Music Listening Lab was a fairly easy credit, this is a much more difficult undertaking. Actually, it's impossible. In our own power we are unable to hear the melody of brokenness. We do not naturally see the depth of our sinfulness. As we have already discussed, our instinct is to hide our brokenness—by justifying our actions, by defending ourselves, or even by trying to be good—all of which result in a superficial experience with God rather than a life-changing one. We cannot hear the melody of brokenness ... without some serious help. Which leads to the good news.

The Spirit of Brokenness

Did you realize that one of the members of the Trinity has this specific ministry written right into His job description? One of the primary ministries of the Holy Spirit in our lives is this: taking the initiative to help us more clearly hear the melody of brokenness, opening our eyes to see and embrace the truth about ourselves. When Jesus was talking to His disciples about the soon-coming Holy Spirit, He described His ministry in this way:

> But I tell you the truth: It is for your good that I am going away. Unless I go away, the Counselor will not come to you; but if I go, I will send him to you. When he comes, he will convict the world of guilt in regard to sin and righteousness and judgment: in regard to sin, because men do not believe in me; in regard to righteousness, because I am going to the Father, where you can see me no longer; and in regard to judgment, because the prince of this world now stands condemned. I have much more to say to you, more than you can now bear. But when he, the Spirit of truth, comes, he will guide you into all truth. (John 16:7–13)

What a powerful description of the ministry of God's Spirit in our lives. Jesus calls Him "the Counselor," which literally means helper or advocate. He is One who comes alongside us for our benefit. This is incredibly good news! God's very own Spirit has been given to us in order to help "guide [us] into all truth," including the truth about ourselves. Jesus says that our Counselor will be actively at work, convicting us "of guilt in regard to sin." The Holy Spirit wants to open our eyes to see the depth of our brokenness—not for the purpose of condemnation but rather for

life and freedom. As we have been saying all along, it is our awareness of our sin and weakness that opens a door for the power of
Christ to be more deeply experienced. God's Spirit is our primary
instructor in our "Gospel Listening Lab."

Now unfortunately, far too many Christ-followers don't really
know what to do with the Holy Spirit. We get the Father concept
and the Jesus thing fairly well. But the Holy Spirit seems a bit
nebulous—and at times even scary. When I was a kid, one of my
favorite movies was *The Ghost and Mr. Chicken* with Don Knotts. It
had the twin elements necessary to terrify a nine-year-old heart—a
scary house and a mysterious organ playing creepy music. So every
time the pastor at church mentioned this "Holy Ghost," it would
give me the creeps. And then when the organ music started ... well,
you get the idea. How interested are any of us in cozying up with
something known as the "Holy Ghost"?

Sometimes we think of the Holy Spirit as being like "the Force"
in *Star Wars*—a very real but basically impersonal power. Jesus is very
clear in His teaching: The Holy Spirit is neither scary nor impersonal. He is the very presence of Jesus in us. Jesus said of the Holy
Spirit: "But you know him, for he lives with you and will be in you.
I will not leave you as orphans; *I will come to you*" (John 14:17–18).
Jesus comes to us in the person of the Holy Spirit. The very Spirit
of Jesus lives in every Christ-follower. We can know Him personally.
We can experience Him intimately.

I often find that Christians, especially Christian leaders, are so
wary of the weird abuses they have seen from those who seem to
focus too much on the Holy Spirit that we unintentionally ignore
His ministry in our lives. We believe in Him; we just don't talk about

Him much—which is tragic. The Holy Spirit is the One who specifically helps us live the gospel, opening our eyes to see the depth of
our need for Christ. Without Him, we tend to minimize the depth
of our sin problem. We don't see how deeply sinful we really are. The
Holy Spirit longs to help us see more clearly.

What then is our part in this process? *Our part is to live with
an open and soft heart toward Him.* That's it. We are to live with
a constant attentiveness to any way in which the Spirit may be
revealing an area of sin *and* a willingness to feel what He feels about
that. An open and soft heart. Both are critical. I can read in the
newspaper about children starving in Africa and not be moved at
all, but when I see pictures on television of real African children in
need, my heart breaks. I am moved to do something. What makes
the difference? The newspaper provides information. The pictures
touch my heart. Genuine brokenness happens not simply by seeing the factual evidence of our sin but by feeling the weight of that
sin as we see it through the eyes of a holy God. The Holy Spirit is
eager to help us *see* that clearly. Our job is to keep our hearts soft
and open.

Spirit Listening Lab

So how does the Holy Spirit help us see the truth about ourselves?
How does He help us hear the melody of brokenness? One of His
most common tools is something that every human being possesses:
a conscience. God has given every one of us a conscience through
which the Holy Spirit can help us see our sin. In Romans 9:1, Paul
defends his words as true by asserting, "I am not lying, my consciences confirms it *in the Holy Spirit.*" The Holy Spirit can use our

conscience to open our eyes to see our brokenness—to see how we are building our lives on things other than Christ.

During one of my son's basketball games, I found myself growing increasingly desirous of victory due to a disdain for the other team's parents who were *so* into the game—unlike me, of course. As I saw how important winning was to them, my cheering became more intense as did my desire for victory. In the midst of this, I began to feel a bit unsettled in my conscience and sensed a question rising in my soul: "Alan, why is this so important to you? Why is winning so important to you?" The very thing I "hated" in the opposing team's parents was just as much a part of me. There in the middle of a sweaty gymnasium, I heard the melody of brokenness as I saw my own soul issues—my own attempt to build my identity on something other than Christ—and I invited Jesus into that place. This was the Holy Spirit at work, using my conscience to help me see my own heart. While I still struggle at times in my level of intensity at sporting events, I now see this struggle differently—as a reminder of my need for a Savior.

Our conscience can be a powerful tool in the Spirit's hands, helping us more clearly hear the melody of brokenness. However, our consciences are not infallible. The human conscience can be weak and immature (1 Cor. 8:7), resulting in a potentially debilitating fear of doing something wrong. It can also be seared and corrupted (1 Tim. 4:2; Titus 1:15) so that awful acts of violence don't bother a person at all.

How then can we ensure that our consciences are appropriately revealing truth in our souls? God has given us a tool for that very purpose: the Bible. The Bible gives us a Spirit-inspired standard whereby we can help discern the accurateness of our consciences. A friend of mine grew up in a home where playing cards and going to movies were deemed satanic evils. Her conscience was extrasensitive to these activities—until the Spirit of God began to open her eyes to the fact that no such prohibition exists in the Bible. Rather than letting our consciences be our guide, we instead let Scripture be our guide as our consciences bring to the surface areas of potential brokenness in our souls.

Living Word

Not only is God's Word a means of checking our consciences; God often uses His Word to awaken our consciences. As we hear the Word taught in our churches and as we prayerfully interact with the Word personally, our eyes are often opened to see areas of sin we have overlooked or been unaware of. I recently taught a weekend message on the subject of prejudice—how it is sinful to treat anyone differently simply because he or she is different from us. The funny thing about prejudice is, no one thinks he or she is prejudiced. No one thinks he or she has a problem with this, which is why I didn't announce the message title the week before or even put it in the program. I was afraid people wouldn't come—not because they didn't *want* to hear the message but because they didn't think they *needed* to hear it. As we gathered that weekend and gave God's Word room to breathe into our lives, the Spirit began to open eyes, including mine, to see something that wasn't even on our spiritual radar a few minutes before. Each of us treats certain people differently or views them negatively because of their differences from us. God used His Word to open our eyes to see the depth of our sin.

Living without an openhearted interaction with God's Word is a lot like living without ever looking at a mirror. Certain parts of your body you can see, but seeing your face requires a mirror. Have you ever had that awful experience of looking at a mirror and realizing that something has been hanging out of your nose for hours? The mirror helped you discover what you by yourself could not see. The author of Hebrews reminds us of the power of the Word. "For the word of God is living and active. Sharper than any double-edged sword, it penetrates even to dividing soul and spirit, joints and marrow; it judges the thoughts and attitudes of the heart" (Heb. 4:12). The Word of God has the power to expose in us things we wouldn't see otherwise—motivations or attitudes that are self-centered rather than godly. The Spirit of God uses the Bible to help us see the depth of our need for a Savior. (In chapter 7, we'll talk in more detail about experiencing the Word in this way.)

Looking under the Hood

Author and counselor Dr. Gary Smalley often describes how our negative emotions are like warning lights on the dashboard of our lives.[1] When a warning indicator lights up on our car's dashboard, the problem is not the light itself. We could take a hammer and break the lightbulb, but that doesn't solve the problem. The purpose of the light is to tell us that something under the hood is not right. Smalley explains that negative emotions like anxiety, anger, or discouragement are actually gifts from God, because they often reveal to us that something under the "hood" of our lives is not right, that something in our souls needs attention. We can either ignore this "warning light" or, with the help of the Holy Spirit, can discover the brokenness under the hood.

For instance, are there people in your life who continually seem to get on your nerves and frustrate you? You could chalk this up to the old "personality conflict" thing, but have you ever considered the possibility that your frustration with this person is an indicator that something in your own soul is out of whack? C. S. Lewis writes, "The point is that each person's pride is in competition with every one else's pride. It is because I wanted to be the big noise at the party that I'm so annoyed at someone else being the big noise."[2] When we feel excessive anxiety over a financial issue in our lives, that anxiety may be God's way of letting us know we are trusting more in our money than in Him. What do our emotions tell us about our brokenness? When in 1998 my favorite college football team lost a game that would have placed them in the national championship for the first time ever, I grieved that loss for months (actually, I'm not sure I'm over it yet). What does that tell me about idols in my own heart?

If, when we experience negative emotions, we are willing to dig a little deeper by asking the "why" question, the Spirit of God can help us hear the melody of brokenness more clearly. In Psalm 73, the psalmist is experiencing some significantly negative emotions as he observes how the wicked crooks around him are prosperous and successful while he struggles to make ends meet. He is bitter and angry, filled with disillusionment and envy, questioning the goodness of God—and then something happens:

> When I tried to understand all this, it was oppressive to me till I entered the sanctuary of God; then I understood their final destiny.... Whom have I in heaven but you? And earth has nothing I desire

besides you. My flesh and my heart may fail, but
God is the strength of my heart and my portion
forever. (Ps. 73:16–17, 25–26)

Notice the psalmist doesn't ignore his emotions, nor does he suppress them. Instead he feels the full weight of them, allowing them to help him see the depth of his need and the greatness of his God. Our negative emotions are a God-given opportunity to hear the music of the gospel more deeply.

Spirituality for Failures

As I look back on my years as a Christian and a Christian leader, I am convinced the greatest source of spiritual discouragement among Christ-followers is the shame of repeated failure—that one area of sin in our lives from which we long to be free and yet we repeatedly fail. Our tempers flare up again; our lust overpowers us again; our fear dominates our thinking again. Frustrated, we wonder, *What is wrong with me?* In the wake of our repeated sin, we become increasingly hesitant to go to the Lord with this because we have failed Him so many times. We feel distant from Him and know that it's our fault. A black cloud of shame hangs over our souls as we feel certain the Spirit of God has left us or at least distanced Himself from failures like us. But has He? Has the Holy Spirit distanced Himself from us? Absolutely not! The Holy Spirit can use our repeated failures to help us better hear the life-giving melody of brokenness—if our hearts are open to Him. We saw in chapter 2 how it was Paul's battle with repeated failure (Rom. 7:14–24) that enabled him to more deeply experience the Spirit (Rom. 8:1–9).

What then is the Spirit doing in our failures? He is helping us see the real problem. A few years ago, my wife and I owned a home that began having sprinkler difficulties. We noticed a leak one day, so we dug up that section and spliced in a small piece of new pipe. A few weeks later, a second leak appeared in another section, and we fixed it as well. When it happened a third time, we decided to dig up the entire linc and immediately discovered several other splice repair jobs done by the previous owner. The real problem was the line itself, which had not been drained during previous winters and was significantly weakened as a result. In order for it to ever work properly, the whole line needed to be replaced.

Often in our areas of repeated failure, we attempt to control the problem by adjusting external behavior, and we never look deeply to discern the sin beneath the sin. For instance, a woman who struggles with gossip might decide on a few strategies to minimize the behavior (pray, bite lip when tempted, reward with a bowl of ice cream for every week without gossiping, etc.) without ever stopping to ask, "*Why* am I so prone to gossip? What need in me am I trying to meet when I gossip about someone else?" The Holy Spirit can help her see the sin beneath the sin. Perhaps her vulnerability to gossip is rooted in her own insecurity—that in order to feel good about herself, she has to put others down with her words. If so, her gossip is actually rooted in a much more significant soul issue—pride and idolatry, both of which are abominations to God! This sin cannot be "fixed" with a few behavioral modifications. It goes much deeper than that—which is why the ministry of the Holy Spirit is so important in our lives. He uses our failures to help us see the depth of our own inadequacy.

If every sin we faced was simply another enemy to conquer and after achieving victory we moved onto the next battle, how aware would we be of our continual need for Jesus? For years, I felt ashamed of my ongoing battle with lust. *If I was really spiritual, I could defeat this thing once and for all.* I now see that my vulnerability to lust is a precious gift from God, for it is a continual reminder of my poverty of spirit—that without Christ I can do nothing. When we view our repeated failures through the lens of a "trying harder" spirituality, we will live under a cloud of shame, continually feeling distant from God. However, when we view our repeated failures through the lens of the gospel, they actually become a blessing in disguise, for they help us hear the melody of brokenness. They serve to remind us of the foundational kingdom value Jesus declared in Matthew 5:3: "Blessed are the poor in spirit."

License to Sin?

Hold it, Alan. Are you saying that failure is a good thing? Should I just go out and sin so that I see my need for Christ? That's a great question— one the apostle Paul anticipates will be asked as he is teaching the gospel to the believers in Rome: "Shall we go on sinning so that grace may increase?" (Rom. 6:1). Same question. In a later chapter, we will specifically address the relationship between brokenness and holiness because they are intimately connected. What I want us to understand here is that the *asking* of this question is evidence you are beginning to truly hear the gospel. The music of the gospel must be far-reaching enough to be heard in the midst of our most shameful failures, or we are not really hearing it at all. There are all sorts of godly reasons to want to walk in holiness, but if our motivation to be holy is rooted in a belief that God won't meet us in our failure, we are missing the heart of the gospel.

There is an incredibly vivid picture of this in Luke 7 as Jesus was dining at the home of a Pharisee named Simon. While they were eating, a woman with a sinful reputation entered the home and began kissing Jesus' feet and anointing Him with perfume. This act of extravagant love troubled Simon a great deal, and he in his own mind began to question Jesus' integrity. Jesus responded to Simon's thoughts by telling him a story:

> "Two men owed money to a certain moneylender. One owed him five hundred denarii, and the other fifty. Neither of them had the money to pay him back, so he canceled the debt of both. Now which of them will love him more?" Simon replied, "I suppose the one who had the bigger debt canceled." "You have judged correctly," Jesus said.
>
> Then he turned toward the woman and said to Simon, "Do you see this woman? I came into your house. You did not give me any water for my feet, but she wet my feet with her tears and wiped them with her hair. You did not give me a kiss, but this woman, from the time I entered, has not stopped kissing my feet. You did not put oil on my head, but she has poured perfume on my feet. Therefore, I tell you, her many sins have been forgiven—for she loved much. But he who has been forgiven little loves little." (Luke 7:41–47)

He who has been forgiven little loves little. In other words, if you don't see the depth of your sin, you will never experience the depth of Jesus' love. If your battle against this recurring sin is a battle to remove the distance between you and God, you don't understand the gospel or the work of God's Spirit. The sinful woman knew the depth of her failure and had experienced Jesus there. Her failure was the doorway into a deeper experience of Jesus' love. For Simon, however, his "successful" spiritual performance was the very thing that kept him from the love of Jesus. When through the ministry of the Holy Spirit we are confronted with the reality of our repeated failure, we are actually closer to God than we ever realized.

The Gift of Confession

As I have been growing in my understanding of the gospel, I have wondered at times as to the purpose of confessing our sins to God, as commanded in 1 John 1:9: "If we confess our sins, he is faithful and just and will forgive us our sins and purify us from all unrighteousness." If our relational status before God is completely dependent upon Jesus' work on the cross, then our sin can't impact that relationship in any way. His love and acceptance of us are a gift given to us permanently in Christ. In the past, I have been taught that my sin hinders my fellowship with God, but if that is the case, what about all the sins of which I'm not even aware and yet am guilty? Either our relationship with God is completely dependent on Christ or it's completely dependent upon us—but we can't have it both ways. So why then are we to regularly confess our sins to God?

Could it be that confession is a gift from God, enabling us to more clearly hear the melody of brokenness? In confession, we take full responsibility for our sin and in doing so see afresh how desperately we need a Savior. Without confession we too easily lapse into a self-sufficient, superficial spirituality—where we are less and less aware of how deeply we need Christ today. Perhaps this is why Jesus includes confession in the prayer pattern He gives us in the Lord's Prayer. He wants us to regularly pray, "Forgive us our sins" (Luke 11:4), not because there are sins of which we haven't been forgiven, but rather because we so easily drift toward independence rather than the gospel.

Now in 1 John 1:9, we are told that our confessing sins results in a "cleansing." To what kind of cleansing does this refer? I don't believe this cleansing changes God's view of us in any way. It is not a restoring of our fellowship with God since our sins are completely forgiven at the cross. It is, however, a cleansing that benefits us—a cleansing of our "new covenant" hearts that can easily become infected by the sin of our flesh. This cleansing opens a door for us to more fully love and embrace Jesus by faith.

When we, like the psalmist, regularly open our hearts to God and pray, "Search me, O God, and know my heart.… See if there is any offensive way in me" (Ps. 139:23–24), the Holy Spirit will answer by showing us in specific ways the depth of our need. One morning during a prayer time with God, I had spent most of my time confessing to Him a sin I had committed the previous day. Over and over again, I admitted my guilt and asked God to forgive me for this sin. After several minutes of this, I sensed the Holy Spirit gently asking me a question: "Is that it? Is that the *only* sin you need to confess?" I started thinking about the previous day—how impatient I had been with my children, my lack of compassion toward someone who was hurting, my feigned listening to someone when my mind was somewhere else.

I realized my one "big" sin was simply the tip of the iceberg in terms of sin in my life. Now you might think this revelation was depressing. Actually, it filled my heart with joy, because I was acutely aware of how desperately I needed a big Savior. Confession opened the door for me to hear the melody of brokenness.

Isn't it awesome to think that God so wants us to live the gospel that He has given us His own Spirit to help us hear the melody of brokenness more clearly? Whether it's through our emotions, our consciences, our failures, or our confession, He is actively working to help us see that we are big sinners in need of a big Savior. That truth opens a door for real transformation … as we will see in the next chapter.

For Personal Reflection/Response

- Write down three or four words that describe your current experience with or attitude toward the Holy Spirit. Now write three or four words that would describe the kind of relationship with Him you desire to have.

- Think of an area in your life (a relationship, a work situation, etc.) in which you consistently experience a negative emotion. Ask the Holy Spirit to show you the root of this, and then engage Him in prayer about it.

- Think of an area of repeated spiritual failure in your life. How has it affected your sense of "closeness" with God? What do you usually hear in the midst of that failure? What might the Holy Spirit want you to hear?

✳ ✳ ✳

Holy Spirit, I long to know You more fully.
I ask You to deepen Your work in my life—not only
increasing my experience of Jesus but also helping me see
more clearly the depth of my sin. I confess that I too often
ignore the ways You long to speak to me about my need for
a Savior. Give me a soft and open heart that is constantly
attentive to You. Help me see in increasing ways how
desperately I need a Savior. In Jesus' name, amen.

Chapter Five

God's Biggest Priority

Be a sinner and sin strongly, but more strongly
have faith and rejoice in Christ.
—Martin Luther

Mark was a young, successful businessman. At thirty-eight years old, he had grown his own business through hard work and a genuine caring for people. But all was not well in Mark's world. During lunch one day, he shared with me about his growing dissatisfaction of soul. He knew something wasn't right but couldn't quite put his finger on it. Having been raised in the church and confirmed in his faith as a teenager, Mark was open to the possibility of there being a spiritual dimension to his struggle. But what was that exactly?

As we talked about what it was that was driving his need to succeed, God began to open his eyes to see how much of his life was fueled by a longing for significance in the eyes of people and a desire for financial security. He was trying to find his life in something other than Christ. As the real desires in his heart were being exposed by God's Spirit, he was broken. Tears formed in his eyes as he said to me, "I am so messed up. I am so far from God. How did I get here? Is there any hope for me?"

I told him the truth. "Mark, I know it feels like you are moving backward spiritually, but you need to understand something. At this moment, you are closer to God than you've ever been. You are closer to God's heart right now than you were a month ago, a year ago, five years ago, even twenty years ago. You have never been closer to God than right now."

I could see the doubt in his eyes. He didn't feel close to God. How could it be that he was closer than ever before? The reason is that for the first time Mark began to see the depth of his sinfulness. That vision opened a door in his soul that had been shut and locked for years. Sure, Mark had long believed Jesus had died for his sins, but now Mark realized how desperately he *needed* that forgiveness, how desperately he needed a Savior.

A Big Savior for Big Sinners

How big of a Savior do you need? Seriously. How big of a Savior do you need in your everyday life? If you are a little sinner (i.e., you mess up periodically but for the most part are doing pretty well), then you need a little Savior. You need a Jesus who can help you when you really mess up, but otherwise your spiritual life is on track. A lot of Christians live their lives as if they need only a little Savior and as a result experience only a little of the gospel's power. The power of the gospel is experienced most deeply by big sinners who need a big Savior.

This is why the first four chapters of this book are so important. Perhaps as you read them, you began to see more clearly how deeply self-centered and self-righteous you can be—how often you look for significance and security in something other than Christ, even good things. Perhaps you began to realize you are a lot more sinful than you ever imagined, and that realization has made you feel increasingly depressed and far from God. Perhaps you are wondering, "Is there any hope for me? Maybe I should just ditch this Christianity thing altogether. It's too hard. I fall so far short."

I've got good news for you. *You are exactly where God wants you to be.* You are closer to Him than you have been in a long time. You are closer to experiencing genuine Christianity than you perhaps have ever been. Why? Because it is our realization of the depth of our weakness and sin that opens a door for us to experience something absolutely wonderful. The very presence of Christ. Paul describes this so powerfully in 2 Corinthians 12:9–10 when he states, "Therefore I will boast all the more gladly about my weaknesses, so that Christ's power may rest on me.… For when I am weak, then I am strong." How's that for a paradigm shift? When we are weak and painfully aware of our brokenness and sin, we can experience Christ more deeply!

Tim Keller, senior pastor of Redeemer Presbyterian Church in New York City, often describes the reality of living the gospel as the simultaneous embracing of two critical truths:

> *You are a lot more sinful than you ever dared believe*
> *and a lot more loved than you ever dared hope.*

These two truths together capture the heart of living the gospel. Yes, we are far more sinful than we ever realized, but that awareness opens a door for us to personally experience the presence of Christ in deeper ways.

The Connection to Christ's Power

So what exactly is it that connects these two realities—the depth of our sinfulness and the presence of Christ? What is it that enables us to experience the sufficiency of Christ in the midst of our weakness and sinfulness? I believe it's faith. Faith is what unleashes the power of Christ in us so we can live in the joy and freedom of the gospel. Even as I write these words, my gut tells me many of you will respond the same way I would have responded before my own "gospel awakening." *Of course! I know that. I know that faith is absolutely critical to the spiritual life. What's so earth shattering about that?* But our typical understanding of faith is way too small for big sinners.

For years, I understood faith to be essentially about two things: First, how we enter into Christianity. When people realizes they are separated from God because of their sin and need Jesus to be their Savior, they are to repent of their sin and place their faith in Jesus, who died on the cross for them. Second, I understood that faith is the response we as Christians are to have when facing difficulty. Whether it is a need for physical healing or the strength to endure hardship, we are to pray boldly and trust God in that situation. Both of these expressions of faith are important, but they are not the complete picture. For many years, I faithfully taught my congregation these two expressions of faith—but I was missing a third critical dimension: *being continually connected to the sufficiency of Christ in the midst of our need.* Rather than simply an entry point or an occasional necessity, faith becomes the essence of the spiritual life. In our constant awareness of our brokenness, faith enables us to tangibly unite with One who is not broken so that we experience His power and presence more fully. This is the heart of what it means to *live* the gospel.

From First to Last

One of the most important descriptions of the gospel is given to us in Romans 1:17, a verse that transformed Martin Luther's understanding of spirituality and resulted in the Protestant Reformation. Luther was a devout monk who sincerely wanted to please God yet was continually overridden with guilt, acutely aware of his spiritual failure. He would literally spend hours every day confessing his sins. One day while Luther was dutifully reading the Bible in the midst of his despair, he read this verse from Romans—a verse he had read dozens of times before. But this time, he really heard it. "For in the gospel a righteousness from God is revealed, a righteousness that is by faith from first to last, just as it is written: 'The righteous will live by faith'" (Rom. 1:17).

What Luther suddenly understood was that our righteous standing before God (i.e., our acceptability before God) is in no way dependent upon how hard we try to be spiritual. The gospel reveals a totally new way to experience acceptance by God—the way of faith. When we place our trust in Jesus rather than in our own effort, we are given the gift of total acceptance by God. Now some of you are thinking, *Come on, Alan. I already know this. This is nothing new. We are saved by faith.* But that's not all Paul is saying here. Listen to this verse again and notice the nature of this faith that Paul describes: "For in the gospel a righteousness from God is revealed, a righteousness that is by faith *from first to last, just as it is written: 'The righteous will live by faith'*" (Rom. 1:17).

"From first to last … the righteous will live by faith." I had read this verse dozens of times, yet I'd never seen that Paul is not simply talking about faith as the means of becoming a Christian. He is talking about faith as a way of life: from first to last. To live the gospel is to *continually* hear the melody of faith, living in constant dependence upon Christ. This kind of faith is absolutely critical to our experiencing genuine spirituality. In fact, let me state this even more strongly: Faith is the one thing God is most interested in from you. Your faith is more important to Him than your worship, obedience, prayer, evangelism, you name it. Now please hear me. I'm not saying these other things are unimportant. They are important, but here's the deal. All of them *proceed* from faith. Faith is the foundation for any and all of those activities. It is the basis for our continual experience of the spiritual life.

It's Everywhere!

A few years ago I was looking to purchase a new car and stopped into a local dealership. As the salesman was showing me around, I saw a car I had never seen before. "What's that?" I asked. He told me the name of the vehicle and began describing it in more detail. I was hooked. I knew I wanted that car. As I drove home to tell my wife, I suddenly began seeing this car everywhere. Lots of people were driving this vehicle. I hadn't seen it before, but it was actually there all the time. That's exactly how it was for me and this whole "faith" thing. Once I realized what Paul was saying in Romans 1:17, I began to look at other passages and quickly discovered it's everywhere! Everything in the spiritual life proceeds from faith. Everything.

In Genesis 15:6, it is Abraham's faith that is commended and becomes a model to us of living the gospel (see Rom. 4:1–3). The entire book of Exodus is a picture of a God who is actively working to deliver His people and to daily provide for their needs. All He wants from His people is that they trust Him. He longs for them to live by faith (see Ex. 14:13). This is God's frequent message to His people throughout the Old Testament: "Trust me" (see Ps. 37:5; Prov. 3:5–6; Isa. 26:4; 30:15). Jesus continues this theme in the New Testament. In John 6:28–29 we read, "Then they asked him, 'What must we do to do the works God requires?'" Notice the question: What *work* does God require us to do? In other words, how can we please God? "Jesus answered, 'The work of God is this*: to believe* in the one he has sent'" (John 6:29). Believing. This is the work God requires from us. Faith. Everything else flows from faith, including our obedience. In Romans 1:5, Paul says that his ministry is "to call people from among all the Gentiles to *the obedience that comes from faith.*" For Paul, faith was the key to his everyday experience with Christ. He writes in Galatians 2:20, "I have been crucified with Christ and I no longer live, but Christ lives in me. The life I live in the body, *I live by faith in the Son of God,* who loved me and gave himself for me." The aged apostle makes it very clear that spiritual growth is not about us trying hard to be holy. It's about us more fully embracing Jesus in the midst of our brokenness. It's about living by faith.[1]

Pleasing God?

When we truly begin to understand that faith is what God is most interested in, it radically changes our perspective on the spiritual life. The church's usual line of teaching is that our main goal in life is to please God, right? We hear sermons and read books urging us to "make God smile" by living lives that are pleasing to Him. What could be wrong with that? Isn't pleasing God a worthy objective? Certainly! Paul writes in Colossians 1:10, "And we pray this in order that you may live a life worthy of the Lord and may please him in every way." Or, in 2 Corinthians 5:9, "So we make it our goal to please him, whether we are at home in the body or away from it." The Bible clearly encourages us to please God; however, the critical issue is *how* we please God. How do we go about living lives that are pleasing to God? We find the answer in Hebrews 11:6: "And without faith it is impossible to please God." Listen again—"Without faith it is *impossible* to please God." We cannot please God without faith. This means that any worship, obedience, good deed, or loving action that we do apart from faith is not pleasing to God.

Why is this? It's because any activity done apart from faith is ultimately rooted in one of two things: pride or fear. Both of these are very subtle and at times can feel quite spiritual, but neither is rooted in the gospel. Take pride for instance. How often is our obedience motivated by a desire to make sure God still likes us or to impress Him with how wonderful we are? Is our ministry to the poor, for instance, motivated by genuine compassion, or is it fueled by how good we feel about ourselves after serving in that way? I admit, it's subtle but significant. Any good thing I do to somehow feel more worthy of God's acceptance is ultimately rooted in pride—the idea that I can do something to get God to feel better about me.

And what about fear? How often is our obedience to God fueled by a fear of disappointing or displeasing Him? Here's an example. Years ago during a bus ride to a high school retreat, I was visiting with one of the leaders who was driving the bus. He made the comment to me that when we drive over the speed limit, we are not pleasing God and, because of that, we remove ourselves from His protection and blessing. It sounded so spiritual at the time. But now I realize, it reeks of a gospel-less spirituality. Sure, it may get me to drive the speed limit, but what's my ultimate motivation? Fear. Fear of punishment, fear of disappointing God. Is that the motivation that is to drive our spiritual lives?

Absolutely not, which is where faith comes in. Rather than pursuing a spirituality rooted in *our* performance and the fear of punishment ("Try hard and hopefully, if you do well enough, you can please God"), we are invited to place our faith in something completely different: *God's* performance and His unfailing love. Jesus already paid for all of our failures by dying on the cross. This means that we experience God's pleasure not by trying hard to please Him but by trusting in His Son. That trust is not just for salvation. It is a way of life, choosing to trust moment by moment in the sufficiency of Christ. That faith decision opens the door for us to experience the presence of Christ flowing through us in a powerful way. It frees us to obey—not because we have to or as a way to make God smile. Instead, we have a completely different motivation.

The Power of Trust

In Tolkien's *The Fellowship of the Ring*, we see a vivid picture of this difference. The movie centers on a magical ring—one that can bestow absolute power on whoever wears it. The ring is a vivid image of sin, because whoever gets near the ring begins to be controlled by it. The ring awakens the sinful nature within people. During one particular scene, Bilbo Baggins, who on an earlier adventure came into the ring's possession, is being asked by his good friend and wizard Gandalf to give it up.

Gandalf: "I think you should leave the Ring behind, Bilbo. Is that so hard?"

Bilbo: "Well no … and yes! Now it comes to it, I don't feel like parting with it, it's mine, I found it, it came to me!"

Gandalf: "There's no need to get angry."

Bilbo: "Well, if I'm angry, it's your fault!" [caresses the Ring] "It's mine! My own, my precious."

Gandalf: "Precious? It's been called that before, but not by you."

Bilbo: "Argh! What business is it of yours what I do with my own things!"

Gandalf: "I think you've had that Ring quite long enough."

Bilbo [puts up his fists]: "You—want it for yourself!"

Gandalf: "Bilbo Baggins! Do not take me for some conjurer of cheap tricks. I am not trying to rob you. I'm trying to help you."

[Bilbo starts weeping. He stumbles towards Gandalf, who embraces him gently.]

Gandalf: "All your long years we've been friends. Trust me as you once did, hmm? Let it go."[2]

Notice, Gandalf's appeal is not "Let go of the ring because it's the right thing to do" or "Just do it because you're supposed to" or even "Do it because I told you to." No. His appeal is rooted in trust: "I'm trying to help you.… Trust me as you once did." It was Bilbo's trust in Gandalf that ultimately broke the stronghold the ring had in his life. Such is the power of faith. It breaks through strongholds that willpower and trying hard cannot break. Jesus extends this same appeal to us every moment of our lives: Will you trust Me? Will you place your confidence not in your own ability but in Mine? That's the only way the power of sin will be broken in our lives. That's the only way we will experience the life God wants us to know. He continually asks us: Will you trust Me?

Two Paths

Two very different pathways are placed before us in terms of our spiritual lives—one is rooted in self-sufficiency, the other in Christ sufficiency. I once heard John Lynch, pastor of Open Door Fellowship in Phoenix, Arizona, describe these two paths.[3] I've tweaked his illustration a bit to apply it specifically to our discussion. He encourages us to imagine ourselves standing at a fork in the road, facing two different pathways to the spiritual life. One path has a sign that says "Pleasing God." The other path has a sign that says "Trusting God." Which path do you choose? You may not like the choice because you want to do both, but you can take only one path.

If you take the Pleasing God path, you come to a door upon which is written "Striving." You take hold of the doorknob of Self-effort and enter the room of Good Intentions. The person on this path desperately wants to please God and is striving to live a life that reflects that desire. However, Lynch points out the danger of this path is that our vocabulary will inevitably turn into "What must I do to *keep* God pleased? How do I *keep* God happy so that my life works?" That is where the Pleasing God path will always lead—more striving, more effort to try to keep God happy with us. It's exhausting. It's never enough. We can never do enough to please God. Many sincere Christians find themselves on this path and can't imagine any other way to do the spiritual life. But there are some who are on this path and realize deep down this is not working. They long for a spirituality that is not rooted in fear, guilt, and drivenness.

Thankfully, there is another route to choose at the fork in the road. The Trusting God path leads us to a door upon which is written "Brokenness." As you take hold of the doorknob of Humility, you enter into the room of Grace—God's undeserved and unending love and favor poured out upon you. There are others in the room who are broken and sinful, just like you, and yet there is no competition or condemnation. The focus is on Christ and His sufficiency. As you experience the fullness of His grace, which is not dependent upon your ability or your performance, you are invited to lean upon Him more and more. In that dependence, you discover the very power and sufficiency of Christ flowing through you. You are freed to follow. Fear and guilt are no longer your motivation. Love is.

Two paths with very worthy objectives, but only one results in pleasing God; ironically, it is not the Pleasing God path! When we choose the path of Pleasing God, we end up neither pleasing Him nor learning to live by faith. Our spiritual lives are dependent upon *our* ability to follow. But when we choose the Trusting God path, continually admitting our brokenness and humbly embracing the sufficiency of Christ, we experience both trusting God *and* pleasing God. Our spiritual lives are not motivated by guilt, fear, and shame but by love, desire, and gratitude. Two paths ... very different results. In the powerful words of Robert Frost, "I chose the road less traveled, and that has made all the difference." This choice truly does make all the difference in our lives.

Which path are you on? Is the primary focus of your life pleasing God or trusting God? Is your confidence in *your* ability to please Him or in *Christ's* ability? That is a huge question that we need to be asking every moment of our lives. Beware: Self-effort and self-sufficiency are always lurking at the door of our hearts. They can creep into our spiritual lives at a moment's notice and distract us from living by faith—which ultimately will hinder God's work in our lives. It's no wonder that faith is God's biggest priority for us.

Pictures of Faith

Okay, Alan, I get it. I understand the importance of living by faith, but quite honestly, I'm not really sure what it looks like in real life. Great point. What exactly does living by faith look like? How can we grow in our experience of this? That's what the rest of this book is about, but let's be very clear. Defining "faith" is no easy task. Faith, by its very nature, can't be reduced to some trite formula. So how do we get a better handle on this?

Perhaps an illustration will help: Imagine standing at a scenic overlook, gazing upon an awesome panoramic view of a mountain range. You long to capture a picture of this so that your friends at home can "see" it, and yet as you look into the viewfinder of your camera, you can view only a portion of the landscape. The lens isn't wide enough to capture it all. What do you do? You decide to begin at the far left and take a photo, then move the camera a bit to your right to take another, then another until the entire view has been captured. Later, you piece together the photos so that the entire view is revealed.

Faith is a bit like that. Trying to define what "living by faith" looks like is very similar to trying to capture a panoramic view with one camera. You can't portray the essence of faith with one image or one phrase. It is too glorious and far reaching. Thankfully, God's Word has given us several snapshots of faith, each of which offers a unique perspective that when combined with the others provides a very powerful and life-changing vision of "living by faith." So let's gaze through our viewfinder in the next few chapters as we examine in detail four specific and God-given images of faith: resting, remaining, gazing, and drinking.

For Personal Reflection/Response

- Name one area of weakness in your life. What would it look like to boast in that weakness, seeing it as an opportunity to more deeply experience Christ? Try to be as specific as possible.

- Which pathway do you most often choose—the Pleasing God path or the Trusting God path? Do you have any idea as to why that is your usual path? How does that feel?

- What is one way your relationship with God would be different if your obedience was rooted in a simple trust in Jesus rather than in a pride in your own worthiness or in a fear of disappointing God?

Heavenly Father, thank You for helping me realize that in my weakness, Your power can be more fully displayed. I desire to embrace my weakness and welcome the fullness of Your presence. I admit my tendency to rely upon my ability and performance rather than the work of Your Son. Jesus, You are an awesome Savior, sufficient for my every need. I long to live my life simply trusting You, rather than trying in my own effort to please You. Grow my faith in You. In Your sufficient and wonderful name, amen.

Chapter Six

Resting in Christ

Cease striving and know that I am God.
—Psalm 46:10 (NASB)

In repentance and rest is your salvation,
in quietness and trust is your strength.
—Isaiah 30:15

In his well-known, humorous stories about Lake Wobegon, Garrison Keillor often refers to a church located in his fictional community—"Our Lady of Perpetual Responsibility." That's a pretty accurate description of the spirituality many people experience, embracing a gospel of perpetual responsibility—striving to please God, to produce more, to grow spiritually. Not surprisingly, this approach to the spiritual life can look extremely successful in Christian circles, but it eventually takes its toll.

The Weariness of Striving

As a young boy, Hudson Taylor opened his heart to Jesus, placing his faith in this crucified Savior. During his teen years, he began to feel God calling him to serve as a missionary to China. At the age of twenty-two, he responded to that call and for the next fifteen years faithfully served God by giving himself wholeheartedly to ministry in China. To those who observed his ministry, he was a model of spiritual maturity and fruitfulness, of diligence and devotion to Christ. But all was not well in Hudson's soul. In a letter to his mother, he opened up his heart to her:

> My own position becomes continually more and more responsible, and my need greater of special grace to fill it; but I have continually to mourn that I follow at such a distance and learn so slowly to imitate my precious Master. I cannot tell you how I am buffeted sometimes by temptation. I never knew how bad a heart I had. Yet I do know that I love God and love His work and desire to serve Him only in all things. And I value above all things that precious Savior in Whom alone I can be accepted. Often I am tempted to think that one so full of sin cannot be a child of God at all; but I try to throw it back, and rejoice all the more in the preciousness of Jesus, and in the riches of that grace that has made us 'accepted in the Beloved.' ... But oh, how short I fall here again! May God help me to love Him more and serve Him better. Do pray for me. Pray that the

Lord will keep me from sin, will sanctify me wholly,
will use me largely for His service.[1]

Do you sense the weariness? Hudson loved his Savior and longed
to please Him but was increasingly aware of the depth of his sin. He
was trying hard and yet falling short. He longed to serve God better,
but he felt like a failure. Was he? As we have been saying all along,
he was exactly where God wanted him. His heart was open to hear
God's invitation to begin living the gospel.

One day, Hudson received a letter from a fellow missionary
friend who described a very powerful spiritual awakening that had
recently occurred in his life. As Hudson read this letter, something
dramatic happened within him. His eyes were opened to see a new
spiritual pathway—one that was not rooted in pleasing God but in
something else. This is what the letter said:

> How do we get faith strengthened? Not by
> striving after faith but by resting in the Faith-
> ful One.... To let my loving Savior work in me
> His will.... Abiding, not striving or struggling;
> looking off unto Him; trusting Him for present
> power; trusting Him to subdue all inward cor-
> ruption, resting in the love of an almighty Savior,
> in the conscious joy of a complete salvation....
> This is not new, and yet 'tis new to me. I feel as
> though the first dawning of a glorious day had
> risen upon me. I hail it with trembling, yet with
> trust. I seem to have got to the edge only, but of

a sea which is boundless; to have sipped only, but
of that which fully satisfies. Christ literally all
seems to me now the power, the only power for
service; the only ground for unchanging joy. May
He lead us into the realization of His unfathom-
able fullness.[2]

Hudson would later admit it was that first two sentence of this
letter that exploded in his heart: "How do we get faith strengthened?
Not by striving after faith but by resting in the Faithful One." Not
striving but resting. Up to that point, Hudson's spiritual life had
been about striving—striving to walk in holiness, striving to please
God, striving for greater faith. All of that left him weary and yet still
longing to do better. What a miserable place to be.

Not long ago, I was visiting with a counselor friend and was
describing my recent weariness of never being able to do enough,
never being able to keep everyone in the church happy. After listening to me for a bit, she said, "Imagine that going on and on for
eternity. Sounds a bit like hell, doesn't it?" I had to agree. It is miserable to always be striving to please God and yet never getting there.
The goal is never reached. I could always do more and do it better. Is
this the life God wants us to live?

Thankfully, no. The life God invites us to live is a life of faith,
and as Hudson Taylor discovered, that faith experience is not achieved
through striving but resting. God invites us to continually experience
the incredible joy of rest in Him, the result of which is tremendous
fruitfulness—the fruit we were longing for but not experiencing.
Those closest to Hudson Taylor said that after his "resting" revelation,

he was never the same. He exuded peace and joy no matter how burdensome his ministry.

Jesus' Invitation

In Matthew 11, Jesus gives us a beautiful picture of what it looks like to live by faith. "Come to me, all you who are weary and burdened, and I will give you rest" (Matt. 11:28). To those who are weary of striving, who are burdened by the reality of never doing enough, Jesus offers rest. Now quite honestly, to many of us this idea of rest feels so passive, almost lazy. *Are we supposed to sit around and do nothing?* But that is to misunderstand the nature of Jesus' invitation. To rest in Christ is a very active and intentional thing. In fact, to those of us who love to be productive, rest can be a most difficult and strenuous activity. Why? Because it forces us to confront our idols of self-sufficiency.

Think about this: Why is it our default tendency in the spiritual life is toward busyness and striving? Why is it we tend to *feel* God's love for us more when we are doing spiritual things? As we discussed earlier, the reason is we don't feel acceptable to God in our current state. We feel like failures. We feel like we need to work a little harder to get God to smile at us. The burden is on us to *gain* our acceptability. This is ultimately a faith issue, isn't it? In this scenario, upon whom are we placing our faith? Us. Our trust is in *our* ability to fix this problem, *our* ability to make ourselves more acceptable and pleasing to God. No wonder we feel so burdened and are working so hard. Our acceptability before God depends on it!

Into this self-sufficient and self-reliant spirituality, Jesus invites us to do the unthinkable—stop working. Stop striving. Stop trusting in your own effort to make God like you more. Instead, come to Him and rest. Choose to trust in the work He has done for you on the cross. That is a work that is finished. It is complete. Nothing more needs to be done in order to earn God's favor or to get Him to smile at us. Do we really believe this? Are we truly resting in the finished work of Christ?

Does God Turn Away?

Many of us believe we are resting in the finished work of Christ, but here's a quick question to help discern whether or not we truly are: When you are committing a willful sin, what do you feel is God's attitude toward you at that moment? What do you imagine God doing when you sin? For many of us, we envision God standing at a distance from us, turning His face away, and saying, "How could you do that again? I'm so disappointed." He's shaking His head in disgust.

For the sake of argument, let's assume He does respond in this way. Let's assume that every time we willfully sin, God turns His face away from us. What then is our motivation for obeying Him? Fear. We're afraid of losing God's grace. We're afraid He'll turn His face from us. We're afraid of disappointing Him, so because of that fear, we choose to obey. Now some would say, "As long as obedience is happening, that's the important thing, right?" Not exactly.

Let's say that you are striving to resist sin because of a fear of disappointing God. But what happens if you fail and willfully give in to some sin? What do you feel? Shame. Distance from God. After all, you've disappointed Him. So what do you do? Here's what I often would do: I'd mope around for a few days, confessing my sin and hoping God would see how miserable I was. Promising God I'd never do it again, I would then throw myself more earnestly into spiritual disciplines. Over time I'd eventually begin to "feel" His smile once more.

But what happens if in a weak moment, we fail *again*? More shame. Deeper shame. We already promised God three weeks ago we wouldn't do this again, but here we are again. God feels even more distant. We feel even more ashamed and inadequate, which often fuels the very sin we are trying to avoid. When we feel inadequate, it's all too easy to turn to things that help us "feel" adequate—food, pornography, shopping, etc.—which only increases our sense of distance from God.

A lot of very sincere Christians are stuck in this shame-based cycle of sin, and they don't even realize it. After all, they are trying so hard to be good. Some are about ready to throw in the towel. This Christianity stuff doesn't seem to be working for them. Do you see what is missing from this equation? The gospel. The gospel says that when Jesus died on the cross, He took *all* of our sin upon Himself— not some of it or most of it. All of it. Not only that, as Jesus hung on the cross, He experienced the horror of absolute separation and isolation from God, crying, "My God, my God, why have you forsaken me?" (Matt. 27:46). At that moment, God the Father turned His face away because He couldn't look upon sin. Think of what this means: Jesus fully experienced the Father turning His face away so that we wouldn't have to experience that ever again. Jesus bore our shame so that we would never have to be ashamed before God again. Jesus experienced distance and alienation from God so that we would never have to be distanced or alienated from God again. That, my friends, is incredible news. That's the gospel! If we think any sin we ever commit, willfully or not, causes God to distance Himself from us and turn His face away from us, we're missing the wonder of the gospel.

Now often this raises a question: What then does it mean in Ephesians 4:30 when Paul urges us to "not grieve the Holy Spirit of God" with our sin? I believe that the grieving described here is similar to the grieving of loving parents whose teenage child is making poor decisions that will lead to negative consequences. The parental grief is not a response of disgust, disdain, or relational distance but rather is a sadness at the pain their child may experience as a result of these decisions. The parents' love toward their child is often intensified in this situation. In a similar way, God grieves our sinful choices and the pain they may bring to our lives, but in no way does this impact His love or relational proximity to us. In the gospel, God's passionate and limitless love for us is never withheld for any reason.

Transformed by Rest

To live by faith is to so rest in the finished work of Christ that we are no longer motivated by a fear of disappointing God or the shame of having Him turn His face away. Our trust is not in our ability to follow God but in the finished work of Christ. To hear the melody of faith is to constantly rest in His unfailing love for us—a love that never turns away or withdraws from us. It is this love that has the power to transform us in a way that fear and shame never could.

How does this transformation happen? Let's return for a moment to the question I asked earlier. What is God doing when we sin? If we believe that whenever we willfully sin, God is standing at a distance, hiding His face from us in disappointment, we will be motivated to obey out of a sense of fear and duty—which will never result in an internal transformation. Guilt and fear work as effective short-term motivators, but they can never transform a heart.

But let me offer a different picture. What if, while we are sinning, the Holy Spirit is whispering to our souls, "I love you. I am always with you. Do you really want to do this? Will this really satisfy and bring life? You and I both know the pain and hurt this will cause. Do you really want this? Trust me. Let it go." Do you feel the difference between these two perspectives? Both may encourage obedience, but only one is rooted in the finished work of Christ. Fear and shame may motivate for a while, but eventually spiritual exhaustion will catch up to us. To rest in the constant love of our Savior brings a transformation of soul that frees us to love, to obey, to worship, to give—but not out of a sense of duty but desire. Such is the power of living by faith.

The Battle for Rest

The word *rest* by definition implies a life of ease, but ironically the spiritual rest Jesus is inviting us to experience is anything but easy. It is a battle that is constantly being waged at the core of our beings. As we saw earlier, two very real enemies of rest—self-sufficiency and self-righteousness—are always lurking nearby. In the book of Galatians, Paul paints a vivid picture of this battle for rest, using a word that is often misunderstood by many Christians. It's the word *flesh*. This word is most often translated "sinful nature" (as we saw in chapter 2) and refers to the evil desires within us. But the word has a much broader meaning than that. In Galatians 3:3, Paul writes, "After beginning with the Spirit, are you now trying to attain your goal by human effort?" That phrase "human effort" is this same word *flesh.* In Paul's mind, the flesh is not simply that part of us that wants to do evil but rather is that part of us that wants to trust in our own effort and ability to please God. With that understanding in mind, look how Paul describes this battle in Galatians 5:17: "For the sinful nature [flesh] desires what is contrary to the Spirit, and the Spirit what is contrary to the sinful nature [flesh]. They are in conflict with each other, so that you do not do what you want."

I believe Paul is saying the battle we face every moment of every day is not ultimately a question of good versus evil but rather a question of whom we will trust. When we are trusting in our own ability to make God happy and earn His acceptance, we are actually living in opposition to the Spirit of God. The Spirit says, "Hey, if you want to do it on your own, go ahead." He is a perfect gentleman who will not force His influence upon us. The result of our self-trust is, as Paul describes, an inability to do what we most deeply want to do (i.e., please God). But when we choose to rest in Christ's ability—to trust in His love toward us and His power in us—the Spirit is freed to exert His influence in our lives. This is why Paul would conclude in Galatians that "the only thing that counts is faith expressing itself through love" (Gal. 5:6). The essence of the spiritual life is faith … period. Not faith plus sincere effort. Not faith plus our hard work. Not faith plus a holy life. The only thing that counts is faith plus nothing— joyfully resting in the finished work of Christ on our behalf.

Experiencing Rest

How do we increasingly experience this incredible rest in Christ? Jesus gives us the answer in Matthew 11:28: "Come to me … and I will give you rest." Come to Jesus. When fears assail, when repeated failures convince us that God has turned His face away, when we feel pressured by religious duty rather than joyful desire, we can come to Jesus. We can find rest in Him.

Now given the busyness of our lives, how do we remind ourselves of this truth? How can we increasingly live in the reality of resting in Christ? God has actually given us two very tangible ways to build this truth into the rhythm of our lives, to regularly tune our hearts to the life-giving melody of faith.

The Table

It is extremely significant that the night before Jesus was crucified, He gave His followers a very specific practice to regularly and permanently incorporate into their gatherings together: the Lord's Supper. Jesus was very clear in His reason for this. He wanted us to *remember* what He had done for us. "This is my body, which is for you; do this in remembrance of me.... This cup is the new covenant in my blood, do this, whenever you drink it, in remembrance of me" (1 Cor. 11:24–25).

Both the bread and the wine point to the finished work of Jesus on the cross. The bread reminds us of His body being given in our place. The wine (or juice) reminds us of a new covenant with God, one that is based not upon our effort but upon Christ's work. Both of these elements speak of the rest that is ours in Christ. But how exactly do they speak? For years, I understood the Lord's Supper to strictly be a symbol of what Christ has done—a reminder of His work. One day it dawned on me that the very nature of this symbol implies more than simply a reminder. After all, Jesus urges us to drink and eat of these elements, ingesting them into our very beings so that they eventually permeate even our bloodstreams. What had for years been a symbol suddenly became for me an experience—an avenue for the Spirit of God to quicken the truths of the gospel in me.

What this means is that anytime we partake of the Lord's Supper, it is an opportunity for our souls to not only be reminded of but to *taste* more fully of the finished work of Christ on the cross. As Paul described to the Corinthians, "For whenever you eat this bread and drink this cup, you proclaim the Lord's death until he comes" (1 Cor. 11:26). In a very real sense, the Lord's Supper is a God-given means of regularly proclaiming to our souls, *It is finished. The work is done. You don't have to strive to earn God's acceptance. You don't have to shrink back from God in the shame of recent failures. You can rest in Jesus, who made you acceptable and who took your shame.* We need that reminder ingested into our souls on a regular basis, don't we? No wonder Jesus established this as a consistent part of our spiritual experience on this earth. No wonder Paul in verse 26 urged us to do this regularly "until he [Jesus] comes." Until Jesus returns, we will never outgrow our need to be reminded of the rest that is ours in Christ.

The Sabbath

In addition to the Lord's Supper, God has given us another very practical means of hearing the melody of rest. It is known as the Sabbath. We often tend to downplay the importance of the Sabbath, but it is clearly a very important thing to God. It is one of the Ten Commandments, right alongside the commands to worship God alone and to not murder or lie.

> Remember the Sabbath day by keeping it holy. Six days you shall labor and do all your work, but the seventh day is a Sabbath to the LORD your God. On it you shall not do any work, neither you, nor your son or daughter, nor your manservant or maidservant, nor your animals, nor the alien within your gates. For in six days the LORD made the heavens and the earth, the sea, and all that is in them, but he rested on the seventh day. Therefore the LORD blessed the Sabbath day and made it holy. (Ex. 20:8–11)

The Sabbath principle of rest is rooted in God Himself. He Himself rested on the seventh day and has set apart one day a week for us to rest—to do no work and to enjoy Him. While some people get hung up on whether or not Christians are to celebrate the Sabbath on Saturday or Sunday,[3] I believe this misses the point entirely. Taking a day each week to rest and enjoy the Lord is a wonderful gift from God—a tangible reminder that our identity is not to be wrapped up in how much work we can do or in how many things we can produce. While any discussion about keeping a Sabbath is often met with resistance and accusations of legalism—some of which is warranted—I'm quite certain that our difficulty in experiencing a real Sabbath has little to do with a fear of legalism and much to do with our need to produce in order to feel valued and important.

Why is it most of us have such a hard time refraining from any work for a twenty-four-hour period of time? Why is it so hard for us to go a day, or even an hour, without taking a work-related cell phone call or without checking our e-mail? Why do solitude and silence make us so nervous and uncomfortable? The answer is simple. While work can be a good thing, we easily turn it into a "god" thing. It becomes the thing from which we derive our identity and value. The more we produce, the more valuable we are. The more our cell phone rings, the more important we feel. Our inability to keep a Sabbath is often an indication of a much deeper issue in our souls—in whom are we trusting for our identity? Are we resting in the sufficiency of Christ and His value of us, or are we determining our value based upon our ability to produce?

This is why having a real day of spiritual and physical rest one day a week is so important for us. It is not a legalistic command we must keep in order to please God. On the contrary, it is a life-giving gift that can enable us to more clearly hear the beautiful melody of faith. The Sabbath is a weekly opportunity to tangibly rest in Christ, to experience afresh in the depth of our beings the reality of an *it is finished* spirituality—one that is not dependent upon our effort. When Jesus said, "It is finished," He really meant it.

Jesus invites us to come to Him and rest—to place our trust not in our own effort but in His finished work on the cross. In learning to rest, we more deeply hear the melody of faith and experience its freedom.

For Personal Reflection/Response

- Let's say that today you started living with a constant awareness that God's face is always toward you and that He never looks away in disappointment. How might things be different within yourself? What might be different at work? How about in a relationship with a friend?

- Try a Sabbath experiment this next week. For an entire twenty-four-hour period of time, do absolutely no work or anything that makes you feel productive. During that time, be aware of the various emotions and sensations you experience—negative and positive. It may be beneficial to write them down. What do those things reveal about your soul?

✳ ✳ ✳

*Jesus, I long to take You up on Your invitation
to come to You and rest. I admit that so much of my life
is built upon self-sufficiency and productivity. I admit
that my feeling of closeness to You is often rooted in my
own performance rather than in Your work on the cross.
Help me learn to rest fully in You—in the aftermath
of failure or success, in the midst of busyness or solitude.
Thank You that "It is finished." I long to know that
more deeply in my soul. In Jesus' name, amen.*

Chapter Seven

Impacted by the Living Word

Let the word of Christ dwell in you richly.
—Colossians 3:16

Most every Christ-follower, when asked, will readily assert the importance of the Bible in the Christian life. There is no question that it is of utmost significance. In John 15:7, Jesus makes it clear that our living by faith is intimately connected to the Word of God in our lives. "If you remain in me *and my words remain in you,* ask whatever you wish, and it will be given you." The word *remain* means to live in or to continuously dwell. Jesus is giving us a vivid picture of faith—to let the Word of God dwell deeply in us. Sounds great, doesn't it? Few Christians would argue this point.

However, there is a deep, dark secret that many of us carry in our souls but are too terrified to admit to anyone: The Bible bores us. We know we are supposed to read it and be excited about it, but whenever we make time to do just that, we feel like we don't get anything out of it … and then we feel guilty for feeling that way. What a frustrating dilemma. Why do we struggle so much in connecting with God's Word?

A Purposeful Interaction

Let me propose that one of the main reasons for this common struggle is a misunderstanding of the purpose of the Word. What is our primary objective when we spend time reading or studying the Bible? What's our goal? That's a really important question that's easily and often overlooked—and the implications are staggering.

Take the Pharisees, for instance. We have talked about how devoted these guys were to God's Word. They knew the Old Testament backward and forward, memorizing and teaching it to other people, as well as earnestly desiring to follow it in their own lives. They were Bible studs—no doubt about it. But listen to what Jesus once said to them: "You diligently study the Scriptures because you think that by them you possess eternal life. These are the Scriptures that testify about me, yet you refuse to come to me to have life" (John 5:39–40). Notice the problem—these religious experts had lots of head knowledge about God's Word, but they missed the whole point of His Word—Jesus. To the Pharisees, the Scriptures were simply rules to live by. To memorize the Scriptures was to *know* how to live. For them, the power of the Word was in the knowledge of what to do. But is that the power of the Word in our lives? Is the Bible simply a guidebook for living, showing us what to do in various situations? A lot of Christians think so.

For many Christ-followers, the Bible is a book of principles to show us how to live. No wonder we struggle to spend time in the Word—how excited are you about spending time reading a to-do list that's 1,500 pages long? When we view the Bible primarily as a book of principles for living, we miss the point. The point of the Bible is not principles but a Person. Jesus said in John 5:39, "These are the Scriptures that testify about me." *He* is the point. If our interaction with the Word isn't resulting in a deepening intimacy with Jesus, a deepening experience of His love and grace, we are missing something huge.

As I mentioned in an earlier chapter, during my college days I was very disciplined in my interaction with God's Word. I spent time in the Bible daily. I met regularly with my pastor to learn how to study the Bible more effectively. I led Bible studies and did some teaching in a Christian ministry on campus. At one point, I remember deciding to memorize the entire book of Philippians ... which I did. I knew the Word. I could quote it and teach it. I had the principles of the Bible down cold—and my soul was cold as well. Somehow I had been led to believe that knowing the principles equated with knowing the Person. It didn't.

The purpose of the Word is to point us to Christ. The Bible is an incredible grace gift from God to us, a living and active document that can move us into a deeper faith experience with Jesus. When the Holy Spirit is ministering to us through the Word, He will always point us to Christ, helping deepen our love for and dependence upon Him as well as our experience of His love for us. Now certainly the Bible contains principles for living, but as we have been saying all along, our adherence to those principles is to be rooted in our faith in Christ, embracing His sufficiency in our inadequacy. Our ability to follow the principles comes from a vital trust in Jesus. So when we approach the Bible primarily as a book of principles, we miss the gospel. We miss an opportunity for our faith in Jesus to be deepened. We miss Jesus.

As a person who teaches the Word of God, I had a troubling realization a few years ago: My preaching tended to be focused on giving people *principles* from the Bible about how to live rather than offering them the *person* of Jesus. The principles provide the "what"; Jesus provides the "how." I still teach principles from the Bible about loving people, giving, obeying—but now, after explaining the principles, I try to make it clear that in our own power, we are unable to follow those principles. We can't do it. Trying hard won't work. In that realization of our brokenness, I then point people to a Savior who is all-sufficient and who desires to live His life through us.

In this way, the Bible provides so much more than principles. It does show us the behaviors and attitudes that should characterize our lives, but it also shows us our inability to do those things apart from faith in Jesus. In Scripture, we see not only the depth of our depravity but also the glory and wonder of our Savior:

> For we do not have a high priest who is unable to sympathize with our weaknesses, but we have one who has been tempted in every way, just as we are—yet was without sin. Let us then approach the throne of grace with confidence, so that we may receive mercy and find grace to help us in our time of need. (Heb. 4:15–16)

That's our Savior. That's the One to whom everything in the Bible points—which radically impacts the way we interact with Scripture.

Information or Encounter?

Let me ask you this: When you read the Bible, are you reading for information or encounter? There is a huge difference between the two. Can you imagine reading a "Where's Waldo?" book without looking for Waldo? You could certainly try, but it would sort of miss the point. In a sense, the Bible is a "Where's Jesus?" book from God to us. God wants us to earnestly seek an encounter with the living Christ in the pages of Scripture. If we are simply reading it for information, we're missing the transformation it can bring into our lives. I mean, how often is your life significantly impacted by reading the newspaper? When we read the Bible like we read a newspaper, we miss the point. We miss an encounter with Christ.

I love the passage in Luke 24 where Jesus, after His resurrection, joins two of His followers as they are traveling to Emmaus, but He doesn't let them know it is Him. After they describe the recent events in Jerusalem—the crucifixion of their leader and the rumors of His body missing—Jesus begins to explain to them the meaning of these things. "And beginning with Moses and all the Prophets, he explained to them what was said in all the Scriptures concerning himself" (Luke 24:27). Notice, "all the Scriptures"—including everything in the Old Testament—point to Jesus. He *is* the point.

Now eventually Jesus reveals to these two men who He really is. Listen to how they later describe this whole experience: "Were not our hearts *burning within us* while he talked with us on the road and opened the Scriptures to us?" (Luke 24:32). This is a vivid description of what can happen in our souls as we encounter Jesus in the Word. Our love for Him can be rekindled; our appreciation of His love for us can be deepened. Our awareness of our own sin can be heightened as well as our awareness of His complete sufficiency. Even when reading the Old Testament, our souls can be pointed to Jesus as we see in the Law God's holy standard and as we see in the behavior of God's people our total inability to meet that standard. Over and over again, we realize how desperately we need a Savior and how grateful we are that we have One. In all of Scripture, Old and New Testaments, we can encounter Jesus. The result? The volume of the gospel's music is heard more deeply in our souls, which makes us *want* to trust Him more.

I remember that when I was engaged to Raylene, we were separated by several hundred miles as I attended school in another state. I longed for her letters—not primarily for the information but more for the glimpses of who she was and the expressions of her love for me. Quite honestly, how gushingly she signed the letter meant as much to me as anything else in the letter. When we begin seeing the Bible as a context for a personal encounter with Christ, it can radically impact our motivation and desire to spend time in the Word. It's not a textbook. It's a love letter.

A Lost Art

Once the desire in our souls is stirred to encounter Christ more deeply in the Word, a natural question arises: How? How do we do this? How do we connect with God's Word in such a way that we hear the melody of faith more clearly? Thankfully God has given us a powerful description of what this looks like and the impact it can have in our lives. It's found in Psalm 1, which is often described as the gateway to the Psalms but is actually more than that. It is a gateway for us into a deeper encounter with the Bible.

> Blessed is the man who does not walk in the counsel of the wicked or stand in the way of sinners or sit in the seat of mockers. But his delight is in the law of the Lord, and on his law he meditates day and night. He is like a tree planted by streams of water, which yields its fruit in season and whose leaf does not wither. Whatever he does prospers. Not so the wicked! They are like chaff that the wind blows away. (Ps. 1:1–4)

The psalmist is painting a vivid word picture of a person whose life is being significantly impacted by the Word of God. Rather than following the ways of the world and being blown here and there like chaff in the breeze, this person is like a tree planted by a stream of water that provides constant nourishment year-round. It's a picture of health and stability. Now what is it that makes the difference between our lives being like chaff or like the tree? It all boils down to our level of engagement in the Bible.[1] We are told that this person's delight is in God's Word. There is a significant longing for a deeper connection with truth—which as we have just discussed is rooted in our desire for Jesus. He is the One we are ultimately looking for in the Bible.

But there is more than just desire. The psalmist explains that this desire is coupled with a particular activity: meditation. Now don't freak out. For many Christians, the word "meditation" is a bit intimidating and possibly even a bit weird. It perhaps brings to mind images of incense and lotus positions, or it makes us think of an ultradeep level of spirituality reserved for a few select introverts with lots of time on their hands. But the practice of meditation is actually quite normal and easily accessible to the rest of us. It is a life-giving tool given to us by God, enabling His Word to more deeply remain in us.

The word "meditation" used in this passage literally means "to mutter, to muse, to whisper, to speak." It is the activity of mulling something over in your mind in such a way that it begins to speak into your soul. It is to chew on some truth until it begins to influence your way of thinking and behaving, because it has penetrated to the core of your being. Sound simple? It should. The truth is, all of us meditate … regularly. When pondering a significant decision such as purchasing a new car or house, we spend days, weeks, even months mulling this over in our minds, processing the input of friends, family, magazines, experts, etc. We're thinking about it as we are waiting at a stoplight. We're processing it as we're trying to sleep. We're discussing it at the dinner table. There is nothing superspiritual about meditation. We're doing it all the time. The critical issue, of course, is *what* we are choosing to mull over and process, *what* we are choosing to let sink into the core of our beings. Whatever that is, it will begin influencing the decisions we make, the attitudes we have, and the way we live.

What we are really talking about is the heart. From a biblical perspective, the heart is that part of us that houses our will, our emotions, and our intellect. It is the location of our passions, our values, and our loves. Because of that, the heart is where our primary decision making occurs. People can *say* they value all sorts of things, but a quick look at their checkbooks and their schedules reveals what they truly treasure. Whatever is in our heart determines the trajectory of our lives—which is what makes biblical meditation so powerful. It is to intentionally let the truth of God's Word—the staggering reality of our brokenness and the incredible love of our Savior—increasingly penetrate our hearts so that our decisions and attitudes more and more reflect the heart of God. It changes the way we perceive reality, which radically impacts how we live.

Distorted Images

Have you ever thought about the messages you hear in the background of your mind? *You'll never amount to anything. God couldn't love you after what you've done. And you call yourself a Christian. No one likes you. You're a loser.* Often these messages penetrate our souls because of some events in our distant past. We think we'll just grow out of them, but often they end up driving our lives. We spend our lives trying to look a certain way or trying to achieve a certain level of success so that we can prove these messages wrong. But we soon find that the voice never shuts up. It continues to influence us from the core of our beings.

How can we ever be free from this? It's by letting a different voice penetrate more deeply in our souls—the voice of God's truth. *You are loved absolutely. You are precious to God. You are His forever. Your sin has been paid in full.* Meditation enables these wonderful truths from God's Word to drown out the old messages that keep you in bondage. It enables you to speak to your soul words that bring life and freedom. Did you realize that you can speak to your soul? Listen carefully to David's words in Psalm 42:5 and 11: "Why are you downcast, O my soul? Why so disturbed within me? Put your hope in God, for I will yet praise him, my Savior and my God." Notice what David is doing. He is talking to his soul. He is speaking words of truth to his heart in the midst of his own discouragement. That's what biblical meditation is—intentionally taking time to speak to our souls God's truth, hearing the melody of the gospel more deeply.

Some Practical How-to's

So how do we do this? Given the fact that we are meditating on something most all the time, how do we become more intentional about meditating on God's Word? The operative word here is *intentional*. In Psalm 1, the writer describes a person who "meditates day and night," which speaks of a consistent and regular practice. There are actually many ways this can happen in our lives. The key is in creating contexts in which we can consistently hear or read God's Word and then mull it over in our minds and hearts.

One of the simplest ways is by regularly sitting under biblical teaching that consistently captures the heart of living the gospel rather than simply offering a list of more things to do. This involves listening with a discerning heart, running whatever you hear through the filter of brokenness and faith. How does this message help you see in a deeper way your need for Christ? How does this message help you more deeply trust in the incredible sufficiency of your Savior? Obviously our local church is the foundational context for this to happen, but we can supplement with other teaching as well. A friend of mine listens to messages on his MP3 player as he is driving to work. I happen to enjoy listening to Bible teaching while I'm exercising. These are simple ways to build into our lives contexts in which we interact with God's Word.

Another context in which meditation can happen is in a small group or mentoring relationship, where we process a passage of Scripture together with other believers. There is something uniquely powerful about the dynamic of authentic community, in which we are openly wrestling with a text and thinking through its implications in our lives. We need each other in order to more fully understand God's heart. Let's be honest—when reading a passage of Scripture, we all tend to focus on things that we are passionate about and easily skip over issues that don't float our boat. A friend of mine is passionate about social justice and ministry to the poor—areas that I tend to skip over. It is through my relationship with her that I am made more aware of the hundreds of verses in Scripture that describe God's heart for the poor.

Personal Connection with God

In addition to these avenues for meditation, there is one more context that I believe is critically important to build into our lives: personal time alone with God and His Word. For me, I experience the presence of Christ most deeply and tangibly in my times alone with Him. The Word of God plays a critical role for me in that time with God—but in what way? I have already mentioned how for years my personal interaction with God's Word was not about an encounter with Christ but information. So how did the Bible become more real to my soul?

Several years ago, I discovered a devotional practice that has enabled meditation to become a regular part of my experience with God. I'd like to share this with you, not because this is the *only* way to do this, but because this is a way that has worked for me. Often I find that Christians *want* a deeper personal encounter with the Word but don't know how or where to begin. If that describes you, then hopefully the next few pages will be helpful as I describe my own practice and then give you an opportunity to experience it yourself. Once you have tried it for a while, you can adapt it to make it your own.

Here's what I have done for a number of years: I have built into my routine a few times a week in which I can be alone with God—no phones, computers, or other distractions. For me, early morning works best. Before I begin, I take an empty chair and set it a few feet in front of me so that it's facing me. This is a tangible and constant reminder to me that Jesus is here and is wanting to meet with me. It reminds me that my purpose is not information but encounter with the living Christ. I begin by asking the Holy Spirit to speak to me from the Bible, and then I prayerfully read a day's portion from *The One Year Bible*.

The One Year Bible is a Bible specifically divided into 365 readings. Each day has a reading from the Old Testament, New Testament, Psalms, and Proverbs. Since my objective is not about getting through the Bible in a year, I don't worry about the date on the page. I simply keep a bookmark that marks my location. It takes me about a year and a half to go through the entire Bible—which is fine with me. Utilizing *The One Year Bible* removed for me one of the biggest barriers to getting in God's Word: not knowing where to read. I used to get so frustrated because I would make time for the Lord, but then I wouldn't know where to start—Old Testament? New Testament? It became paralyzing and discouraging for me. I talk to so many people who struggle with this same thing. They want to interact with the Bible but don't know where to start. Using *The One Year Bible* in this way has removed that burden.

Because my goal is *encounter* with Christ rather than simply getting information, as I read I try to be attentive to the Holy Spirit "highlighting" for me a phrase, a verse, or a small passage—something that stands out to me and catches my attention. As mentioned in chapter 4, it may be an area of brokenness I need to confess. It may be an area of truth I need to stand on. It may be an attribute of Jesus I can appreciate and enjoy. More often than not, there is something that stands out in the passage. When that happens, I will stop and chew on it a little bit, mulling it over in my mind, letting it speak to my heart. I frequently turn it into a prayer right then—"God, thank You for being so merciful," or "Jesus, may You increase and I decrease," or "God forgive me for my lack of compassion. I need You to express Your love through me." In this way, the Scriptures become the fuel for my connection with God rather than simply being driven by my own agenda.

Specific Examples

Let me give a couple of examples of what I'm talking about: Not long ago, I was reading in Colossians 3, which describes how we are to set our hearts and minds on Christ. It's a passage that is fairly familiar to me, and yet as I was reading one particular verse, three words seemed to jump out at me. *"For you died,* and your life is now hidden with Christ in God" (Col. 3:3). *For you died.* I started to chew on that a bit. I repeated it a few times and then made it personal. *I have died. My life is not to be about Alan Kraft but about Jesus Christ.* In that moment, I confessed to the Lord how often my life is focused on my glory, not Jesus. I realized afresh that living by faith means dying to my self-absorption, so that I can set my heart on Christ. This all happened in a period of a minute or two, but my soul was fed as Jesus became more real to me. After that morning, there were other times that phrase came to my mind: "For you died, Alan." It was a truth that continued to nourish my soul and point me to Jesus.

Another example: Recently, my Old Testament readings for several days were from the book of Judges, which is one of those books in the Bible that is downright disturbing—the violence, the wickedness, and the evil make you want to scratch your head and ask, why is this in here? So I'm reading about a guy who lets his wife be raped all night by the men of the town who actually wanted to have sex with *him*. When she dies as a result of the violence perpetrated against her, he cuts her body into pieces and sends it to various places in Israel to let them know what had happened. They respond with horror and attempt to exact justice for this crime, which results in several thousand men dying in battle. What do you do with a passage like this? Where is Christ found in these pages of Scripture? I discovered Him in a sentence scattered throughout the book, including its final verse: "In those days Israel had no king; everyone did as he saw fit" (Judg. 21:25). What is most frightening about the book of Judges is that it exposes what we all are capable of when we do whatever seems right to us. That morning, as I read of these ancient horrors, I was reminded of how skewed my life becomes apart from Christ and how desperately I need Him today and every day. It moved me to offer a prayer for mercy.

Sometimes rather than a verse or phrase, God uses an entire story to speak specifically into my life. A few years ago, I was in the midst of a leadership fog, uncertain about the direction of our church. Some leaders had expressed concern about a spiritual apathy in our church body, but I was unconvinced and put their thoughts on the back burner. A few days later during my time with the Lord, I opened my *One Year Bible* to my bookmark and began reading the Old Testament passage. It was the story of Asa (2 Chron. 14—16), who early in life had humbly sought the Lord in the midst of a difficult battle, and God dramatically answered. But later in his life, after years of an absence of difficulty, he found himself in a similar situation and this time tried to fix it himself. He established a treaty with a neighboring nation rather than turning to God. As I read this passage, it came alive to me, and I knew God was speaking to me and to our church about the danger of spiritual complacency when things are going well. I hadn't wanted to believe it but now knew it was true. I scrapped my sermon for the week, sensing this was God's message for our church—a call to break out of our spiritual complacency and seek God afresh. It was a significant turning point in our church family, one that many people still recall. And to think, it occurred because of a passage I "happened" to be reading during a devotional time with the Lord.

Most of my personal times in the Word are not that dramatic, but I can honestly say that more often than not, a verse or phrase will capture my attention as I am reading and prompt me to stop and meditate on it in such a way that it nourishes my soul in that moment. It has energized my devotional life, knowing that the Holy

Spirit is so eager to speak. On those occasions when I read the entire passage and nothing seems to stand out, I may go back through and look more attentively or may simply transition to my time of prayer.

How About You Try It?

Why not take a few minutes and try what I have been describing? Below you will find a reduced portion of an actual day's reading from *The One Year Bible*. Get in a quiet place alone with God, and begin with a simple prayer, asking Him to speak. Then dive in and see what happens.

Portion of *One Year Bible* Reading, March 28

DEUTERONOMY 10:6–22

6 (The Israelites traveled from the wells of the Jaakanites to Moserah. There Aaron died and was buried, and Eleazar his son succeeded him as priest. 7 From there they traveled to Gudgodah and on to Jotbathah, a land with streams of water. 8 At that time the LORD set apart the tribe of Levi to carry the ark of the covenant of the LORD, to stand before the LORD to minister and to pronounce blessings in his name, as they still do today. 9 That is why the Levites have no share or inheritance among their brothers; the LORD is their inheritance, as the LORD your God told them.)

10 Now I [Moses] had stayed on the mountain forty

days and nights, as I did the first time, and the LORD listened to me at this time also. It was not his will to destroy you. 11 "Go," the LORD said to me, "and lead the people on their way, so that they may enter and possess the land that I swore to their fathers to give them."

12 And now, O Israel, what does the LORD your God ask of you but to fear the LORD your God, to walk in all his ways, to love him, to serve the LORD your God with all your heart and with all your soul, 13 and to observe the LORD's commands and decrees that I am giving you today for your own good?

14 To the LORD your God belong the heavens, even the highest heavens, the earth and everything in it. 15 Yet the LORD set his affection on your forefathers and loved them, and he chose you, their descendants, above all the nations, as it is today. 16 Circumcise your hearts, therefore, and do not be stiff-necked any longer. 17 For the LORD your God is God of gods and Lord of lords, the great God, mighty and awesome, who shows no partiality and accepts no bribes. 18 He defends the cause of the fatherless and the widow, and loves the alien, giving him food and clothing. 19 And you are to love those who are aliens, for you yourselves were aliens in Egypt. 20 Fear the LORD your God and serve him. Hold fast to him and take your oaths in his name. 21 He is your praise; he is your God, who performed for you those great and awesome wonders

you saw with your own eyes. 22 Your forefathers who
went down into Egypt were seventy in all, and now
the LORD your God has made you as numerous as the
stars in the sky.

LUKE 8:4–21

4 While a large crowd was gathering and people were
coming to Jesus from town after town, he told this
parable: 5 "A farmer went out to sow his seed. As he
was scattering the seed, some fell along the path; it was
trampled on, and the birds of the air ate it up. 6 Some
fell on rock, and when it came up, the plants withered
because they had no moisture. 7 Other seed fell among
thorns, which grew up with it and choked the plants. 8
Still other seed fell on good soil. It came up and yielded
a crop, a hundred times more than was sown."
When he said this, he called out, "He who has ears
to hear, let him hear." 9 His disciples asked him what
this parable meant. 10 He said, "The knowledge of the
secrets of the kingdom of God has been given to you,
but to others I speak in parables, so that, 'though seeing, they may not see; though hearing, they may not
understand.'
11 "This is the meaning of the parable: The seed is the
word of God. 12 Those along the path are the ones
who hear, and then the devil comes and takes away the
word from their hearts, so that they may not believe
and be saved. 13 Those on the rock are the ones who

receive the word with joy when they hear it, but they have no root. They believe for a while, but in the time of testing they fall away. 14 The seed that fell among thorns stands for those who hear, but as they go on their way they are choked by life's worries, riches and pleasures, and they do not mature. 15 But the seed on good soil stands for those with a noble and good heart, who hear the word, retain it, and by persevering produce a crop.

16 "No one lights a lamp and hides it in a jar or puts it under a bed. Instead, he puts it on a stand, so that those who come in can see the light. 17 For there is nothing hidden that will not be disclosed, and nothing concealed that will not be known or brought out into the open. 18 Therefore consider carefully how you listen. Whoever has will be given more; whoever does not have, even what he thinks he has will be taken from him."

19 Now Jesus' mother and brothers came to see him, but they were not able to get near him because of the crowd. 20 Someone told him, "Your mother and brothers are standing outside, wanting to see you." 21 He replied, "My mother and brothers are those who hear God's word and put it into practice."

Psalm 69:29–36

29 I am in pain and distress; may your salvation, O God, protect me.

30 I will praise God's name in song and glorify him with thanksgiving.

31 This will please the LORD more than an ox, more than a bull with its horns and hoofs.

32 The poor will see and be glad—you who seek God, may your hearts live!

33 The LORD hears the needy and does not despise his captive people.

34 Let heaven and earth praise him, the seas and all that move in them, 35 for God will save Zion and rebuild the cities of Judah. Then people will settle there and possess it; 36 the children of his servants will inherit it, and those who love his name will dwell there.

PROVERBS 12:2–3

A good man obtains favor from the LORD, but the LORD condemns a crafty man. A man cannot be established through wickedness, but the righteous cannot be uprooted.

How was it? Was there a phrase, a verse, or a story that captured your attention? Did you spend a few moments chewing on that phrase, letting its truth seep into your soul? Now imagine the impact if this kind of encounter in the Word was a regular part of your experience with God—if even a few times a week, the Word was being allowed to nourish your soul in this way. I love the image from Psalm 1 mentioned earlier: "He is like a tree planted by streams of water, which yields its fruit in season" (Ps. 1:3). A person who builds into his or her life a regular practice of meditation is like a tree planted by a stream, receiving constant nourishment no matter what the circumstances.

One of the things that makes *The One Year Bible* so powerful in our devotional practice is that it enables the Spirit to speak to us from passages we wouldn't necessarily go to on our own. If we're only spending time in our favorite passages, we may be missing significant things the Lord wants to speak into our lives. Even if we are able to do this routine only a few times a week, we will be regularly and prayerfully interacting with the entire Bible every two years. That means that our souls will be consistently exposed to every word God has spoken in the Scriptures. How cool is that!

Now let me reiterate: Using *The One Year Bible* in my devotional practice has worked well for me, but it may not work for you. For some, it may feel like too much material is covered in each reading. I totally understand. Please don't get bogged down in a devotional practice that doesn't connect with your soul. Remember the goal—*to encounter Jesus in the Word*. Whatever enables you to personally connect with God's Word on a regular basis is a win. You may want to read only the Old Testament portion one day, waiting until the next time with God to read the New Testament portion. Or you may want to use a different tool altogether. Finding your particular routine may take some adapting and experimenting, but it's worth it. The power of any kind of devotional routine is not so much in the dramatic, onetime revelation that blows your socks off. That certainly can happen, but more typical is the quiet and consistent encounter with the living Christ, who over time will feed your soul through His Word, enabling you to increasingly live by faith, trusting moment by moment in this wonderful Savior who has given His all for you. That's life changing!

For Personal Reflection/Response

- What difference is the Bible making in your life right now? Have you set aside regular opportunities for God to speak into your heart through His Word? If not, what might a next step in that direction look like for you?

- If you didn't before, spend fifteen minutes prayerfully reading *The One Year Bible* section on pages 136–140. What words, verses, or passages stood out to you? Take some time to think about its implications for your life, and then turn it into a prayer to God.

✳ ✳ ✳

Heavenly Father, thank You for Your Word,
through which You long to point me toward a deeper
encounter with Jesus. Increase my longing for that as well.
I pray that, as I make time to spend in Your Word,
You would meet me there through the presence of Your
Spirit. Speak into my heart truths that will drive out
the lies I have believed. Open my eyes to see in greater
ways the depth of my brokenness and the wonder
of my Savior. In His name, amen.

Chapter Eight
Gazing upon Christ

Since, then, you have been raised with Christ, set your hearts
on things above, where Christ is seated at the right hand of God.
Set your minds on things above, not on earthly things.
—Colossians 3:1–2

Let us fix our eyes on Jesus, the author and perfecter of our faith.
—Hebrews 12:2

What does it mean to live by faith? As we are discovering, that's
not an easy question to answer. At the end of chapter 5, we saw
that describing what living by faith looks like is similar to trying to
capture a panoramic view with one camera. You can't do it. What
you can do, however, is take individual shots and then piece them
together later. That's what we are in the process of doing. We are
using various images of faith described for us in the Bible to paint
a picture of what living by faith looks like in real life. Now some of

these pictures might overlap on the edges but together provide a wonderful panoramic view.

So far we have seen that living by faith involves resting in Christ and letting His Word remain in us. Both of these images bleed into a third picture of faith that is repeatedly mentioned in Scripture yet rarely identified and embraced by many Christians. We've experienced its power in other aspects of our lives but have probably not viewed it as being that substantial. What is it? The power of a gaze.

Seeing or Gazing?

I'll never forget the moment I met my wife for the first time. It was in the middle of a church service in which I had been introduced as a seminary student doing a summer internship. During the infamous "turn and greet your neighbor" time, I turned around, and there she was. The handshaking and introductions lasted only a few moments, but my world was spinning as I sat back down. Being the spiritually mature intern, I spent the rest of the service ignoring the sermon and instead plotting how I could ask her out as soon as possible. One look and I was hooked.

Seeing is not the same thing as gazing. There were hundreds of people I *saw* that morning, but only one captured my heart and my affections. Now I wish I could say the same for Raylene, but she later admitted that her first impression of me was, "Hmm … typical seminarian. Tall, pale, and skinny." Oh well. It took me awhile to turn her seeing into gazing, but I thank God it eventually happened. Seeing is one thing; gazing is another. Seeing can be fun, informative, helpful—but gazing will change your life.

Simon Peter learned this lesson in a very dramatic way. One

day, in order to speak to a large group of people, Jesus stepped into Simon's boat and asked him to put out a little from the shore. Now this was not the first time Simon and Jesus had met. We learn in Luke 4 that Jesus had previously healed Simon's mother-in-law, so they are certainly acquainted. Simon has *seen* Jesus. After teaching the people, Jesus performs an incredible miracle on Simon Peter's boat, multiplying fish where there hadn't been any before. And suddenly, everything changes for Simon:

> When Simon Peter saw this, he fell at Jesus' knees and said, "Go away from me, Lord; I am a sinful man!" … Then Jesus said to Simon, "Don't be afraid; from now on you will catch men." So they pulled their boats up on the shore, left everything and followed him. (Luke 5:8, 10–11)

Although Peter had previously seen Jesus do miracles, suddenly he sees Him in a new way. Peter sees his own sinfulness in light of Christ's holiness and then experiences Jesus' grace and love extended toward him in his brokenness. The result? He left everything to follow Him. He was no longer simply *seeing* Jesus. He was *gazing* upon Him … and there is a big difference. There are lots of people who are well acquainted with Jesus and even feel a great sense of admiration toward Him … yet have never truly gazed upon Him. One can admire and keep a safe distance at the same time. But one cannot gaze without the soul being stirred. To gaze upon Jesus is to see Him with the eyes of our hearts. It is to see Jesus for who He is and, in that seeing, fall more deeply in love with Him. We see beyond our own inadequacy to His adequacy. We see beyond our sinfulness to His holiness. We see beyond our insufficiency to His sufficiency. We long to more deeply embrace Him and trust Him. It is a life of heartfelt affection, of passionate desire. Nothing else compares to the beauty of our Savior. Our lives become focused on Him.

I love the way the psalmist captures this longing:

> One thing I ask of the LORD, this is what I seek: that I may dwell in the house of the LORD all the days of my life, to gaze upon the beauty of the LORD and to seek him in his temple. For in the day of trouble he will keep me safe in his dwelling; he will hide me in the shelter of his tabernacle and set me high upon a rock. (Ps. 27:4–5)

What an incredible picture of living by faith. The one thing David longed for more than anything else was to gaze upon the beauty of the Lord. There was a passion in his heart to see more clearly the glory of his God. David knew that gaze would completely reorient his life. It would completely rock his world. That's what gazing upon Christ always does—it radically impacts our lives, our perspective, our passions. It transforms us.

In 2 Corinthians 3:18 we read, "And we, who with unveiled faces all reflect the Lord's glory, are being transformed into his likeness with ever-increasing glory, which comes from the Lord, who is the Spirit." The word translated "reflect" can also be translated "contemplate" or "behold," which many scholars agree fits the context better. We are changed, not by *reflecting* God's glory, but by *beholding* it—by gazing upon the beauty of the Lord. Paul says this gaze transforms us in a profound way. It progressively transforms us into God's likeness—but how? What makes this gaze so transformational?

The Power of a Gaze

As we have already discovered, to gaze upon something involves much more than seeing. To gaze is to find ultimate beauty and value in another object in such a way that it significantly impacts our lives. What we often fail to realize is that every one of us is gazing upon something all the time. As humans, we gaze upon anything we deem beautiful, pleasing, or valuable. We set our hearts upon it. We find delight in it. We look for satisfaction in it. It could be our new SUV, our career, a relationship, our appearance, our sexual desires. While we like to think that we are independent creatures, the reality is, we are all dependent upon something else to bring us life. God placed within every one of us a need to gaze, a need to deem something beyond ourselves valuable and necessary. And here's the scary truth: Whatever we gaze upon controls us.

A person who deems business success to be absolutely essential for his own happiness will easily find himself working sixty to seventy hours a week, even though he says his family is most important to him. His gaze is upon his own success. A person who deems the approval of others to be absolutely essential for her happiness may find herself obsessed with dieting and unable to eat. What we gaze upon is what ultimately controls our lives, because it is what we are ultimately trusting in. This is why gazing and faith are intricately connected. To gaze is to trust. So the critical question is not, *will* we gaze upon something? Of course we will. We are constantly trusting in something beyond ourselves to bring us life. The critical question is, upon what or whom are we choosing to gaze? The answer to that question dramatically impacts our lives.

Steve came up to me after a worship service, his countenance revealing obvious distress. "Pastor Alan, my problem is not that I can't see my sin. It's that I see it all too well and feel horrible about it. My whole Christian life is one of beating myself up over past mess-ups and failures. I know God forgives me, but I can't seem to forgive myself." Over the years, I have heard a number of Christians share a similar struggle. Although we understand God's forgiveness, we can't seem to forgive ourselves. Why is that? What exactly does that mean? The answer has everything to do with the gaze of our souls.

When we confess our sin to God and are still unable to forgive ourselves, it means we are gazing upon something other than Jesus for our experience of forgiveness. We are trusting in something more than Him. In my own life, this something is often my self-exalted reputation—my felt need to be perfect in the eyes of others. When we feel a compulsive need to be seen as the perfect spouse, the perfect student, the perfect child, the perfect pastor, it's no wonder we can't forgive ourselves. We are trusting in and gazing upon something that is incapable of forgiveness. Your reputation *can't* forgive you. Only Jesus can. You will never experience the joy of feeling forgiven unless you fix your gaze upon this incredible Savior who gave His life for you. In beholding His glory, we experience real transformation.

This is why the writer of Hebrews, when telling us how to actively resist sin, urges us to "fix our eyes on Jesus, the author and perfecter of our faith" (Heb. 12:2). This is why the apostle

Paul, when warning the Colossian believers to resist religious legalism, tells them to "set your hearts on things above, where Christ is seated at the right hand of God. Set your minds on things above, not on earthly things. For you died, and your life is now hidden with Christ in God" (Col. 3:1–3). And in Isaiah 40, when the prophet is encouraging the people to renew their trust in God, he says to them: "See, the Sovereign LORD comes with power, and his arm rules for him…. He tends his flock like a shepherd…. He brings princes to naught…. He gives strength to the weary" (Isa. 40:10–11, 23, 29). Isaiah desperately wants the people to *see* Him for who He is.

These Scriptures clearly indicate that experiencing the transforming power of living by faith happens in our lives as we choose to continually fix our gaze upon Jesus—to find Him more beautiful, more sufficient, and more satisfying than anything else in our lives. To gaze upon the beauty of Christ is a significant transformational experience because in gazing upon Him, we are increasingly captivated by His glory. Our passion for Him is aroused. Our desire for Him is increased. We long for Him to more fully live His life through us. We are changed in that moment because our hearts are more receptive and open to His influence and fullness in us.

Competing Desires

This all sounds great, but if we're honest with ourselves, we know there are all sorts of other desires that so often capture our gaze. At any moment in time, we are pulled in all sorts of directions—none of which may be toward Christ. Sometimes this battle feels overwhelming. What do we do with these other desires? How do we rid ourselves of their influence? The answer is far simpler than you think.

Thomas Chalmers, a Scottish preacher from the last century, once gave a sermon titled "The Expulsive Power of a New Affection." In this message, Chalmers points out that the only way to lessen the pull of worldly desires in our lives is to have our hearts find a greater desire, an affection that is more captivating than any other desire. We see this reality in everyday life. Let's say you have a teenage son who loves to sleep until noon during the summer. What would it take to motivate him to get out of bed at the crack of dawn? You could try some very pointed lectures warning about the dangers of laziness and extolling the virtues of discipline, but I doubt they would have much impact. However, the moment football practice starts, he is out the door by 6:00 a.m. His strong and seemingly unyielding desire for sleep instantly got trumped by a new affection—winning football games. Is his desire to sleep in gone? Not a chance. He just found something he desires more.

When we focus on squelching and eliminating our worldly desires, we will often find ourselves bruised and weary from the battle. We know how strong these desires are and how difficult they are to get rid of. But when our hearts are truly captivated by the beauty of Jesus, every other desire takes a backseat to Him. The psalmist captures this so powerfully in Psalm 37:4: "Delight yourself in the LORD and he will give you the desires of your heart." When you find exquisite delight in who God is, He in turn places *His* desires in your heart. To gaze upon His beauty opens a door for genuine transformation as you long for more of Him and less of you. Can you imagine the impact of this in your everyday experiences? How would your life be different if your heart was increasingly captivated by the incredible and unending love of Jesus toward you?

In his book *The Wisdom of Tenderness*, Brennan Manning relates the experience of Edward Farrell, who years ago traveled to Ireland to celebrate his favorite uncle's eightieth birthday. On the morning of the birthday, Ed and his uncle got up early and went for a walk along the shores of Lake Killarney. Just as the sun rose, his uncle turned and stared straight at the sunrise. Ed stood beside him for twenty minutes in silence. Then the elderly man began to skip along the shoreline, a radiant smile on his face. After catching up with him, Ed commented, "Uncle Seamus, you look very happy. Do you want to tell me why?" "Yes, lad," the old man said, tears washing down his face. "You see, the Father is very fond of me. Ah, me Father is so very fond of me."[1]

How might your *life* be different if you were increasingly captivated by the love of God the Father toward you? How might your *relationships* with others be influenced if your heart was captivated by the mercy of Jesus poured out upon you? How might your *worries and fears* be affected by a deepening gaze of your soul upon the limitless power and sufficiency of your Savior? How might your *struggle* with greed or lust be impacted if your passion for Jesus were to become a greater reality in your heart? To live by faith is to see Jesus with increasing clarity, to see Him more clearly as a Savior who is far more wonderful than you ever imagined.

Growing in Our Gaze

So how do we grow in this experience of gazing upon Christ? What we need is something to help us be reminded of how beautiful and awesome He is. We need something that can stoke our passion and appreciation for Christ in the midst of daily lives bombarded and easily seduced by competing desires. Thankfully God has given us a simple and yet powerful tool that can help us grow in our gazing upon Christ. That tool is the incredible gift of praise.

Praise can enable us to gaze upon Christ in the midst of everyday life. To praise is to express the truth of how glorious and awesome Jesus is. There are two key parts of that definition. One is the word *express*. Praise is not praise unless it is expressed in some way. I can think of all sorts of wonderful things about my wife, but my thoughts won't impact her unless I communicate these things to her. In the same way, the power of praise is in our decision to express it. Praise can be expressed in a variety of ways. We can speak praise. We can sing praise. We can write, dance, paint, kneel, or raise our hands in praise. But praise is not praise unless we choose to express it to God. The power of praise is in our decision to say it, sing it, paint it, dance it, write it, etc.

The other critical part of the definition of praise relates to the object of our praise. Our expression of praise is rooted in the *truth* about who God is. This is very important to understand. It is not simply what I *feel* about God at the current moment. It is rooted in truth, regardless of how I feel or what circumstance I find myself in. These two elements are what make praise such a life-giving tool in our journeys of faith. Praise is a *decision* we make to express to God the truth about who He is. It supersedes our circumstances, our feelings, our fears, and our doubts. Because of that, it enables us to begin *seeing* Christ more clearly. Praise opens a door for us to more powerfully experience Christ.

There is an amazing example of this in Acts 16 where Paul
and Silas were in Philippi, preaching the gospel. When Paul cast a
demon out of a slave girl who was involved in fortune-telling, her
owner became irate because his source of income was now gone. He
brought Paul and Silas before the magistrates, who decided to deal
very severely with them. They had them stripped, beaten, and then
thrown into a dungeon prison with their feet fastened in stocks.
Can you imagine what Paul and Silas must have been experiencing that evening? Bleeding from their wounds, bound by chains,
humiliated, mistreated, hindered from their ministry, robbed of
their freedom, discouraged, depressed. What would you do in that
situation? My instinct would be to nurse my wounds, gripe about
the injustice, and call a lawyer. Look at what Paul and Silas did:
"About midnight Paul and Silas were praying and singing hymns to
God, and the other prisoners were listening to them" (Acts 16:25).
This is amazing. In the midst of absolutely horrible circumstances,
Paul and Silas are choosing to express praise to God, singing hymns
to Him. As they make this counterintuitive choice, a miraculous
earthquake occurs. Paul and Silas are freed, and their jailor comes
to Christ.

While praise does sometimes change circumstances as in their
example, the real power of praise is that it changes us. It enables us
to see spiritual reality more clearly. It cuts through the fog of our circumstances and enables us in that moment to gaze upon Christ. The
psalmist urges us to "enter his gates with thanksgiving and his courts
with praise" (Ps. 100:4). Praise enables us to enter into the courts of
God, to gaze upon Him more fully. In Psalm 22:3, we are told that
the Lord is "enthroned upon the praises of Israel" (NASB). He inhabits

the praise of His people. When we choose to praise God, it opens a door for us to experience Him more deeply, to see Him more clearly.

A few years ago, I had to have surgery on my vocal cords to remove a very small growth. Needless to say, as a person whose vocation is dependent upon his ability to speak, I was more than a little apprehensive about the surgery. During the thirty-minute drive to the surgery center, my wife and I chose to listen to a CD that had several songs of praise that were precious to us. I remember how, in the midst of my fear, the love of God washed over me as I sang those songs to Him. Praise became a way for me to gaze upon Jesus when my own circumstances were making it difficult to do so.

Remember as a kid being at a parade or some event like that where you couldn't see what was happening because your vision was blocked by all the tall people in front of you? What did you do? You'd pull on your dad's pant leg, feel his arms lifting you up, and suddenly the entire view was yours to enjoy. The people around you no longer captured your attention or caused your frustration. You could see what you longed to see. Praise is a bit like that. In the midst of life's daily challenges and busyness, it is easy for our vision of Christ to be blocked and our desire for Him to wane. But when we choose to praise, when we choose to express to God how awesome He is, it's like pulling on your dad's pant leg and immediately being lifted so that you can see. Suddenly the view looks very different. Your soul is once again reminded of what it was created to gaze upon.

Raw Praise

Now before we go too far down this road, let me clarify something. There are times when I hear some Christians talk about "praising

God" in a way that seems forced and inauthentic. It feels more like a self-help, positive-thinking strategy: Fake it till you make it. The underlying message is clear. *Mature Christians don't feel discouraged. Mature Christians don't ever experience doubt. So don't let anyone know you are struggling. Just paint that smile on your face and keep saying "Praise God" until victory comes.*

I'm not talking about that at all. In fact, that is the antithesis to the gospel we have been describing in these chapters. The gospel frees us to admit our brokenness rather than feeling like we have to hide it from God and others. To choose to praise God is not an invitation into superficiality, squelching what is really going on in our souls. No. It's quite the opposite. God invites us to experience what I like to call "raw praise"—a praise that flows in the midst of the real stuff of life. So where do we learn how to experience that kind of praise? You'll be glad to know that there is an entire book of the Bible devoted to this very thing: the Psalms.

There is something I find very interesting about the Psalms. On one hand, everyone loves this book of the Bible. Most every Christian in the face of a loved one's death will turn to or quote from memory Psalm 23—"The Lord is my shepherd...." Certain psalms have provided strength and encouragement for millions of believers throughout history. But there are other psalms that, quite honestly, make us a bit uncomfortable. We tend to skip over them because they seem incompatible with spiritual maturity, openly describing personal fears, doubts, anger, and discouragement. For instance ...

> Surely in vain have I kept my heart pure; in vain
> have I washed my hands in innocence. (Ps. 73:13)

> Why, O LORD, do you stand far off? Why do you
> hide yourself in times of trouble? … Break the arm
> of the wicked and evil man; call him to account for
> his wickedness. (Ps. 10:1, 15)

> You have taken my companions and loved ones from
> me; the darkness is my closest friend. (Ps. 88:18)

Do you hear the doubt, the frustration, the discouragement, and the anger? The psalmist wasn't interested in putting on a super-spiritual front for God, hiding his negative emotions. No. He was interested in running *to* God with his negative emotions, experiencing them in God's presence. The Psalms give us an amazing insight into what to do with our negative emotions. Rather than trying to stuff our anxiety, doubt, or anger under the guise of being spiritual and rather than running away from God for fear of His displeasure, we can do the unthinkable. Run *to* God with it. Experience it fully in His presence. Acknowledge your hurt, your hatred, your confusion. He knows all about it anyway.

When we do that—when we run to God in the midst of our doubts, fears, anger, or frustration—something amazing can happen. Authentic praise can begin bubbling to the surface of our lives, because we are experiencing God in the midst of our pain rather than despite it. That's when praise takes on a whole new meaning. Our youngest son, Joshua, was born with some very significant special needs that impact his speech, his cognition, and his digestion, among other things. Raylene and I love him so much and long to figure out what is wrong so that we can get him the help he needs.

This search has included a multitude of doctors, specialists, books, treatments, diets, supplements, and healing prayer sessions. While he has shown some improvement, the progress is quite slow. I remember waking up to Joshua's crying early one morning only to discover a massive diaper mess that had occurred while he was sleeping. As I was in the midst of cleaning him and changing sheets, I was so overwhelmed with frustration that I began cussing at God and crying out to Him for not helping my son. After a few minutes of this, I had this thought settle in my soul: "Where else can I go? I don't like what You are doing here, Lord, but there is no one else I would rather run to than You. You are my life and my portion." Praise began to bubble forth in the messiest of places.

The Language of Praise

So how can we grow in our experience of praise so that we more frequently gaze upon the beauty of Christ? I find that one of the biggest barriers to praise being a more significant part of our lives is in not being familiar with the language of praise. Why is it that when most of us are looking for a special greeting card for someone we love, we rarely choose the card that's blank inside? It's because we need some help in articulating our love for this person. We need someone else's words to help us express what is on our hearts. Praise is the same way. We often need help in articulating what is in our hearts, which is why God has given us the Psalms. Not only are they an example of authenticity. They are also a wonderful way to learn the language of praise.

There is a very easy way to begin learning from the Psalms how to praise. It's by incorporating them into our personal time with the

Lord. In fact, this is a very natural part of the devotional practice I described in the last chapter. I already mentioned how I use *The One Year Bible* in my devotional experience. Well, thankfully, every day's reading has a portion of a psalm. This means that every time I am opening my heart to God's Word, I am opening my heart to the language of praise. So here's what this looks like for me. When I get to the psalm portion of my Bible reading, I will simply pray it out loud to God. I'm not talking about simply reading it. I actually pray it to Him, reading it aloud as a prayer to God. Sometimes, certain words strike a particular chord in me, and I will make it my own, adding some of my own prayer to what I have just prayed, like one might add a few sentences at the end of a greeting card to make it personal. For instance, let's say I am praying aloud Psalm 3:3: "But you are a shield around me, O LORD; you bestow glory on me and lift up my head." After praying those words, I might add, "Thank You, Lord, that I can lift up my head in Your presence. I don't have to hide my face from Your gaze, all because of Jesus. I praise You, Lord." In this way, the Psalms can begin to help us learn the vocabulary of praise—not from an ivory tower of sterilized sentimentality, but from the breadth of experience of life itself. We will learn the language of praise in the midst of our joys and sorrows, our peace and anxiety, our love and anger.

Another great help in gazing upon Christ through praise are songs of worship we sing in church or hear on the radio or play on our MP3 players. These songs help give language to what we feel in our hearts toward God. There are often times when, in the midst of driving somewhere or doing some menial chore at home, I hear a worship song being played and my spirit begins to soar.

My heart is filled with gratitude and praise. I wasn't even thinking about God, but the song stirred something in me and helped me gaze upon Christ in that moment. This is one reason why weekly worship attendance is so critical—not in a legalistic sense but because our souls need it. After a week of being bombarded with all sorts of things and having our desire for God squeezed out by other desires, our souls need to gather with other believers and together gaze upon the only One worthy of our praise.

The more we choose to gaze upon Christ, the more fully we experience His beautiful and life-giving presence. As C. S. Lewis describes it, "We do not want merely to *see* beauty, though, God knows, even that is bounty enough. We want something else which can hardly be put into words—to be united with the beauty we see, to pass into it, to receive it into ourselves, to bathe in it, to become part of it."[2] That is our longing and our privilege, as the bride of Christ. We are content not simply to *see* His glory but to *gaze* upon it—to experience His glorious presence fully at work in us. Such is the wonder of this life of faith.

For Personal Reflection/Response

- What are some of the things you "gaze" upon? In other words, what are some of the things you find yourself day-dreaming about? What's the last thing on your mind at night and the first thing to mentally greet you in the morning? What occupies your heart, and from whom or what are you deriving your identity and value? What would it take for Jesus to become the center of your gaze?

- How much of your relationship with Jesus is more about *seeing* than *gazing*? (If this is a little unclear, you may want to go back and read that section again.)

- Slowly pray aloud Psalm 42 to the Lord, perhaps even two or three times. Tune in to the emotions you experience.

✳ ✳ ✳

Jesus, You are beautiful. You are my life and my love.
I don't want to simply admire You from a distance.
I want to gaze upon You in such a way that my life is
forever changed. My fears, my pride, the pull of my flesh …
all consumed by a deeper yearning for You.
Help me to become more fluent in the language of praise,
and may that praise authentically flow from both the pain
of my life as well as the joys. In Jesus' name, amen.

Chapter Nine
Drinking Deeply

Jesus, Thou joy of loving hearts,
Thou Fount of Life, Thou Light of men,
From the best bliss that earth imparts
We turn unfilled to Thee again.
—St. Bernard of Clairvaux

One beautiful fall morning, my wife and I decided to drive up to the mountains near our home to see the aspen trees changing colors. Unfortunately, we got off to a late start because of the various challenges of getting four children ready for school. After stopping for a bite to eat, we realized we were barely going to have time to see any scenery at all. So we hurried into Rocky Mountain National Park and headed to Bear Lake, all the while very conscious of our time constraints. In the midst of the frustration of trying to view the fall colors from a moving vehicle, I finally decided to pull over and stop. We took a few minutes to do something we hadn't really had time to do: Enjoy the view. It was life giving to do so—and we made it home in time to pick up the kids from school.

In all of this discussion about the panoramic view of living by faith, it would be very easy for you to feel compelled to hurry through this or to perhaps feel a bit overwhelmed with this ever-expanding vision. Don't. Instead, enjoy the view. Each image of living by faith is not intended to be added to a comprehensive to-do list for spirituality. We saw earlier how dangerous that can be. Rather, these images reveal how accessible this life of faith really is for ordinary Christians like you and me. We really can experience and enjoy a deepening life of trust in God—even in the midst of the busyness and craziness of life. Still don't believe me?

What if I told you that "living by faith" is similar to something you already do throughout your day, something you do instinctively, automatically—without disrupting your busy schedule? Something like … drinking water, for instance. You can drink water in the middle of an important staff meeting, while experiencing a long commute, or pulling an all-nighter. It's not added to your schedule but becomes a natural part of your daily routine. Could living by faith really be that simple and accessible?

Look carefully at Jesus' words in John 7, as He is describing for a large crowd the essence of the spiritual life:

> On the last and greatest day of the Feast, Jesus stood and said in a loud voice, "If anyone is thirsty, let him come to me and drink. Whoever believes in me, as the Scripture has said, streams of living water

will flow from within him." By this he meant the Spirit, whom those who believed in him were later to receive. (John 7:37–39)

There is nothing complicated about Jesus' description of living by faith. It's as simple as drinking water. "If anyone is thirsty, let him come to me and drink." To live by faith is to come to Jesus and drink of Him. Just as drinking water is a natural and continuous aspect of our day, so too is this experience with Jesus. He is not simply describing a onetime event—coming to Him for the first time. No. Jesus is describing a way of life, a constant experience any and every Christ-follower can have, where as we recognize any thirst in our lives, any brokenness in our souls, we can come to Jesus in that moment and drink deeply of His inexhaustible resources. These resources are constantly available to us through the presence of the Holy Spirit, who, as Jesus says, is a stream of living water flowing in us. The Spirit of Christ makes available to us the very presence of Christ.

What is immediately striking about Jesus' description is the *personal* nature of it. Jesus is not simply asking us to believe some principles; He is inviting us to experience Him as a person. "Come to *me* and drink." In the midst of our busyness, in the midst of stress, in the midst of the stuff of life, we can experience the very presence of Jesus, drinking deeply of His limitless resources. Think about that for a moment—the very presence of God is yours at any moment in time. Now some of you may be thinking, *Alan, I already know that God is with me.* Great, but how *aware* are you of His presence? It's one thing to know intellectually that God is with you. It's quite another to *experience* His with-ness, to drink deeply of His presence throughout your day. That's something that for many of us feels unreachable—but is it really?

The Awareness Factor

Imagine the following the scenario: Every morning, you go to the same off-the-beaten-path coffee shop for a latte and some time to read the newspaper to find out what's happening in the world. One day as you're drinking your coffee, you notice another customer with his laptop, surfing the Internet. At that moment, you realize something you never knew before: Your favorite coffee shop has wireless Internet capability. All this time you have been surrounded by the capacity to connect to billions of pieces of information around the world, yet you were unaware of it. The next morning you bring a laptop, and instantly you have access to every online newspaper in the world.

What changed? The coffee shop didn't change. The only thing that changed was your *awareness* of the reality around you. This new awareness awakened in you a desire to intentionally connect with what was there all along. The same thing is true in our spiritual lives. The reality of Jesus' presence with us is a truth that is asserted repeatedly in Scripture (Matt. 1:23; 28:20; Col. 1:27; Heb. 13:5). The Holy Spirit is continually inviting us to experience this glorious reality of Jesus with us. The critical question is, how *aware* are we of His presence? That awareness can be absolutely life changing.

I remember finding myself engaged in an increasingly volatile conversation with a colleague. There was an intensity and defensiveness on both sides that signaled an unhappy ending to the dialogue.

In the midst of my personal angst, I sent up a prayer of desperation—
"Help, God!"—and immediately sensed the presence of Jesus there
with us. My attitude softened, and as a result there was a noticeable
positive change in the tone and direction of the conversation. It's
amazing what can happen in those moments we become more aware
of Jesus' presence with us.

Author and counselor Dr. David Eckman describes a conversation he had with a Christian young man who had struggled for
years with sexual immorality and pornography.[1] With his marriage
falling apart, he was desperate to be free from the overpowering pull
of sexual sin. After listening for several minutes to this young man
confess and describe his various sexual encounters and pornographic
involvements, Dr. Eckman asked him a question: "Have you ever
shown the centerfold to God?" The young man stared in disbelief.
"I'm serious," Dr. Eckman stated. "Have you shown the centerfolds
to God the Father?" The young man blushed. Though he hadn't been
embarrassed during the previous several minutes as he had described
his various sins, the thought of inviting Jesus into that area caused
him to blush. He had never even considered doing that. Why not?
It's not like Jesus wasn't there with him anyway. Jesus was there seeing
every image, but the shame this young man felt was too great to ever
invite Jesus into that "secret" place. This man was living a life discon-
nected from Jesus in this one area, and the result was a disconnect
from the power of Christ in that area.

Several months later, Dr. Eckman was speaking in a church, and
this young man came up to him, wearing a huge grin on his face and
holding the hand of a young woman. He said, "Remember me? I'm
the guy you told to show the centerfolds to God." He proceeded to

describe how that one question about inviting Jesus into that sin radically impacted his life. He was now experiencing a freedom that he had never known was possible. His marriage had been restored. How did this happen? It happened by doing the unthinkable—by welcoming the presence of Jesus into his sin, weakness, and shame. In that faith decision, he experienced the loving and holy presence of Christ flowing through him.

So often we have areas of our lives in which we have posted a "No Trespassing" sign to Jesus. The guilt, the shame, the fear we feel keep us from ever letting Jesus get near. Ironically and sadly, it is often this shame that will lead us back into the sinful behaviors of which we are so ashamed. Sin always thrives in secret. But imagine what might happen if you choose to come to Jesus in that moment, to welcome His presence as you are raiding the refrigerator, or looking at porn, or exaggerating the truth. What if you choose to be aware of His loving presence in the midst of that sin?

Big Brother Is Watching You

Now I remember as a kid hearing a similar and yet adulterated version of this truth. It went something like this: "Remember, Jesus is always with you, so make sure you are pleasing Him. Would you watch that movie if you knew He was sitting beside you? Would you listen to that music if you knew Jesus was in your room with you?" Sound familiar? That lecture has probably been used on countless teenagers over the years. Perhaps it has even helped some teens avoid some sinful behaviors. So what's the problem with it? Notice what it is rooted in—fear and guilt. "Jesus is watching you, so don't mess up. You don't want to disappoint Him, do you?" It's sounds a bit like

Santa Claus: "You better not cry or pout … because you know who is coming to town." That is not the gospel.

The gospel is not about seeing Jesus as our heavenly policeman who guilts us into obeying. Guilt and fear are pretty effective motivators— short term. They never result in real change. Real change happens as we experience the reality of Jesus' loving presence in the midst of our daily lives. Yes, He is with us as we surf the Net or watch TV or listen to music, but He is not scowling at us no matter what we are doing. He has His loving arm around our shoulders and is whispering to our souls, "I love you and I am here. I am your life. I am what you are looking for. Drink deeply of Me." To welcome the presence of Jesus into our sin allows His love for us to drive out our shame, guilt, and fear. We are freed to embrace the sufficiency of Christ in the midst of our weakness. We are choosing to live the gospel.

What's so cool about this is that this is how real transformation can happen—not by trying harder to get rid of our sin, but by embracing the presence of Christ in the midst of that sin. Think of an area in your life in which you are not living the way you want to be living. For me, I immediately think of my parenting. I long to be a more patient dad. I find myself growing impatient in the middle of a game of Sorry or dominoes if my children aren't doing their turn as quickly as they could. I admit it. I'm a grump when playing games, but I don't want to be. So how can I become more patient? I already beat myself up enough over this, so pep talks to do better don't seem to be working. But what would happen if I welcomed the presence of Jesus into my game playing? What if I became aware of His presence with me? What if Jesus actually played the game *through* me? What would He be doing? Laughing with my children, loving them for who they are—which is exactly what I want to be doing. So I tune in to His presence and ask Him to live His life through me. In that faith decision, Jesus is "freed" to love my children through me. I am choosing to live by faith, to drink from Jesus in the middle of my need.

Do you see how different an approach this is to the spiritual life than we as Christians typically embrace? When facing an area in which we want to experience change, our approach is so often to ask God to change us—to make us more patient, to make us more loving, to make us less prone to gossip. But does this really work? No, because it is not rooted in faith. We want God to change us so that we sin less. God wants us to trust Him ... which *results* in our sinning less. There is a huge difference between those two approaches: One is rooted in us; the other is rooted in Christ.

The "S" Word

There is a large, seminary-sized word often used to describe this. It's the word *sanctification*. Sanctification is the process whereby over time we become more and more like Christ. The moment we initially place our trust in Jesus for salvation, we are *justified* before God, which means we are declared acceptable in God's sight. God sees us as righteous in Christ. Nothing can change that. However, we still struggle with sin and are not righteous in our behavior. There is a disconnect between how God sees us and how we live. The process in which these two realities become aligned is referred to as sanctification. How does sanctification happen?

For years, I believed that sanctification happens as we earnestly practice the Christian life. As we over time participate in prayer, worship, spiritual disciplines, church attendance, relational account-ability, etc., we become more like Jesus.

I don't believe that anymore. The only way I can ever become like Jesus is as I am increasingly allowing Him to live His righteous, holy, merciful, loving life through me. In other words, it is not that my flesh is becoming less sinful over time. It's that I, over time, am seeing in greater ways the depth of my need and am turning more and more to Jesus, drinking of His inexhaustible resources. This means we are not only *justified* by faith; we are also *sanctified* by faith. The only real change you will ever experience in your life is as you allow Jesus to live increasingly His life through you—which is ultimately a faith issue.

In Galatians 2, Paul gives us a powerful picture of what it looks like to drink deeply of Christ. "I have been crucified with Christ and I no longer live, but Christ lives in me. The life I live in the body, I *live by faith* in the Son of God, who loved me and gave himself for me" (Gal. 2:20). For Paul, faith was not an "every once in a while" experience. It was the way he lived his life. In the midst of his constant awareness of his need ("I no longer live"), Paul chose to continually place his trust, his confidence in Jesus, who lived in him. As he chose to continually drink of Jesus' unlimited resources, the very life of Christ was unleashed and expressed in Paul. Jesus Christ was living His life *through* Paul.

Counselor and author John Smeltzer describes this experience in terms of a water pipe.[2] A water pipe always assumes the temperature of the water flowing through it. If hot water flows through a pipe, the pipe gets hot; if cold water flows through the pipe, it gets cold. The pipe cannot *make* itself hot or cold. It is completely dependent upon the water flowing through it. Our spiritual lives are like a water pipe.

Through willpower and self-effort we can't *make* ourselves hot or cold. We assume the temperature of whatever is flowing through us at the time. As we drink deeply of Christ and allow Him to live His life through us, we at that moment *experience* His life-giving temperature. The "spiritual heat" we radiate comes directly from Him. Whenever we stop drinking from and relying upon Him, the "temperature" of our lives becomes lukewarm. Rather than us trying hard to *become* like Christ, we are instead allowing Christ to increasingly live His life through us.

This is how faith changes us. It is not simply that we are trusting Jesus to help us become more holy. No. It is that we are more and more allowing the holiness of Christ to be freely expressed in us. Rather than trying to *be* more righteous, we actually *experience* His righteousness flowing through us. Rather than us trying to *be* more loving, we *experience* His love flowing through us into the people around us. Rather than us trying to *have* more holy desires, we *experience* the holy desires of Jesus. This is what sanctification looks like. This is what it means to drink deeply of Jesus. The more deeply and frequently we drink, the more fully His life is expressed through us.

Increasing Our Awareness

Okay, okay, Alan. I get the concept, but how do I really do this in real life? Thankfully, it's not complicated. It doesn't require long hours in prayer or a master's degree in theology. As I mentioned before, it's as simple as drinking water. Not long ago, I read somewhere that a person my age should drink sixteen glasses of water a day. The next morning I brought to my office a large pitcher filled with water. Throughout the day that pitcher on my desk frequently reminded me of my need, and I would pour another glass and drink. Overall, it was a positive experience—other than having to go to the bathroom twenty-seven times in a period of eight hours.

What I learned from that experience is that my remaining hydrated required some intentionality on my part. It required me to stop periodically—in the midst of my busyness—and become aware of my body's need for liquid, taking a few moments to drink a glass of water. In a similar way, to drink deeply of Jesus is to build into our lives frequent moments in which we intentionally stop and become aware of His presence with us, allowing Him to "hydrate" our souls no matter where we are or what we are doing. This intentionality is what is often referred to as "practicing the presence of Christ."[3]

To practice Christ's presence is to grow in our awareness that Jesus is with us all the time. We can practice His presence anytime, anywhere—while standing in a crowded elevator, while driving on the highway, while changing a diaper, while working in our cubicles, while waiting for some medical test results, while taking an exam, while lying awake at night, or while watching football. (Confession: I've yet to experience that last one; however, I remember once asking author Brennan Manning if he was able to practice the presence of Christ while watching a Notre Dame football game. He said he did. So it must be possible!) We can learn to become more aware of Christ's presence with us anytime and anywhere.

Living in the Present

Most of us long for this kind of connection with Jesus. Why then is it so hard for us to experience? One of the biggest barriers is the simple fact that we so rarely live in the present moment. The busyness and pace of our lives urge us to continually live in the tyranny of the *next* thing: What are we going to do next, what are we going to say next, where we are going to go next. When we're in church, we're thinking about what we'll do after church. When we're at home, we're thinking about work. When in a conversation, we're thinking about what we are going to say next. Whether it's five minutes ahead or five hours, we often tend to live our lives in the future moments rather than the current one.

The other temptation is to live our lives in the past—rehashing what we said to someone yesterday, regretting what we did a year ago, wondering how life could have been different. Whether we are focused on the past or the future, the result is the same: We rarely live fully in the present moment. When I am home in the evening with my family, my wife, Raylene, will at times ask, "So where are you?" My body is there. I may even be making eye contact in a conversation, but she knows that I'm not *present* with her. She senses that my heart and mind are elsewhere—and it disrupts our connection with each other. The only moment that a relationship can be fully experienced is the present.

Think about what that means in our relationship with Christ. Do you want to drink more deeply of His presence? If so, you must learn to live more fully in the present. The only place we can experience Jesus is in the present moment—not five minutes from now or five minutes ago. Right here, right now we can experience Him. But this means we must *learn* how to be present.

How fully do we live in the present? Why don't you try a little experiment? Take the next sixty seconds, and be present in your body by tuning in to one or two of your physical senses. For

instance, touch. Feel the weight of your body on the chair. Feel the
skin of your foot against your shoe. Be aware of what your skin is
experiencing. Or perhaps you would want to focus on your sense
of hearing. Listen for one minute to all the sounds happening all
around you. Hear the air conditioner running. Hear each breath
you take. So go ahead. Try it for one minute. Be present to at least
one of your senses.

How was it? Was it easy? Difficult? Did you begin to taste of
the reality of actually living in the present moment? You can try this
same thing while driving. Rather than letting your mind drift to a
situation at work or home, or letting your emotions be aroused by
talk radio, be present in your car. Turn off the radio, and instead
tune in to where you are at that moment. Notice the things you are
driving past. Be present to your own breathing, present to your own
feelings. If you are anything like me, you will immediately become
aware of how foreign this experience is. We are not used to being
present very often.

Now if you want to go a little further with this practice, try it
with another person. Sit across from someone you know well, and
be present with him or her for five minutes. Describe out loud all
that you see and feel—the tint of the person's hair, the expression
on his or her face, the color of his or her shirt, the position of his or
her hands and legs. Be attentive to your own feelings in the midst of
that—the anxiety about trying this, the warmth you feel toward him
or her. Many people who try this are absolutely amazed at the connection they feel with the person—even in just five minutes! Such is
the power of being present in the moment. It enables us to experience life in that moment.

Of course, the operative word is *practice*. This does not come naturally to most of us given the pace and busyness of our lives. But it is something we can practice and learn so that it becomes a more natural part of our everyday lives, including our experience with Jesus.

Practicing the Presence of Christ

Imagine the impact of this in your relationship with Jesus. What if there were moments in which you were fully present to Him—your mind, your heart, your spirit, your emotions—all completely present to Him. What would that be like to actually *experience* Him? Why not try it? Get alone in a quiet place, and tune your soul to Him. What works best for me is to make it a part of my devotional practice that I described in the two previous chapters. I mentioned that whenever I have time alone with God, I pull up an empty chair and set it a few feet in front of me, as a tangible reminder of Christ's presence with me in that moment. Then during my mediation and prayer time, I try, though not always successfully, to take a few minutes and simply enjoy the Lord, being present to Him.

Now I may make some of you uncomfortable here, but let me be clear—this is not an exercise in "thinking" about God. It is deeper than that. As I mentioned in chapter 7, the Bible fuels our encounters with Christ, but the Bible is not Jesus. Jesus is a person who can be experienced personally. So to be present with Him is to let all of your senses tune in to the reality that He is right there with you. Don't say anything. Don't do anything other than simply enjoy Him.[4] Take three to five minutes and be present to Him. See what happens.

Before you do that, however, let me warn you of something that is almost certain to happen. The first few attempts at this will be extremely frustrating and will feel like abysmal failures. We are so used to constant noise, busyness, and activity that any attempt to quiet ourselves feels unnatural—like instantly stopping a car that's moving forward at seventy miles per hour. Doable? Yes. Easy? No. So when you set aside time for this, be aware that initially your blood pressure may very well rise rather than fall as you try to be quiet and yet find your mind thinking about all sorts of other things. The spot on the carpet you hadn't noticed before makes you think about the last time the carpet got cleaned, which was when you had your friends over for dinner, and you realize you haven't talked with them for a while and you wonder how their daughter is doing…. Five minutes later, you remember you were supposed to be experiencing God! At this point, it is easy to want to give up and leave this for "supersaints." Please don't. What you are experiencing is normal *and* temporary. It will soon dissipate.

One early Christian writer described it this way.[5] When a person is used to having neighbors constantly going in and out of his house, what will happen the day he gets fed up and chooses to lock the doors and windows? Lots of neighbors will be loudly knocking on the door and calling out to be let in. But if he ignores the demands and noise for long enough, the neighbors will eventually wear down and go away. The same is true in our souls. When we first try to be quiet and present with Jesus, the noise in our souls may sound deafening. But don't give up. Be patient and gentle with yourself. Eventually all those distractions that were used to being able to get your attention will eventually go away from neglect. You will find yourself enjoying the stillness and growing in a real experience with Christ. It's not easy initially, but it's well worth it.

Now once you begin to taste of this in your times alone with God, you will then be able to "take it on the road." While getting frustrated waiting in the checkout line at the grocery store, try practicing the presence of Christ. Experience His gentleness at that moment. In the midst of a difficult final exam, take a moment and be aware of Christ's presence with you. Let the peace of His presence drive out your fear. Wherever, whenever—this experience can be ours. We can drink deeply of the very presence and life of Christ. In doing so, we are choosing in that moment to live by faith.

Bubbling Over

Jesus' description here in John 7:37 is a wonderfully succinct summary of the heart of this book—what it means to live the gospel. Anyone who is thirsty (i.e., who acknowledges the depth of his or her brokenness and need) can choose in that moment to trust Jesus, drinking deeply of His presence. That one decision can be absolutely life changing. Listen to how Jesus describes it in the very next verse: "Whoever believes in me, as the Scripture has said, streams of living water will flow from within him" (John 7:38). What an amazing picture of the power of the gospel in our lives! When we live in continual brokenness and faith, something profound happens, not only in us but also *through* us. The lives of those around us will be significantly impacted as well … as we will see in the next chapter.

For Personal Reflection/Response

- Does the thought of welcoming Jesus into *every* area of your life excite you or scare you? Why?

- Jesus says, "If anyone is thirsty, let him come to me and drink" (John 7:37). In what areas of your life are you thirsty? Is this thirst something recent, or have you been thirsty a long time?

- Try the "practicing the present" experiments mentioned in this chapter. Start by yourself. Then try to practice the presence with another person. Finally, try it in your relationship with God.

✳ ✳ ✳

Jesus, I am thirsty for You. Often I live my life
in the past or in the future, rather than in the
present moment. Because of this, I miss out on a deeper,
life-giving connection with You. I want and need
Your presence to flow in and through me every moment of
my life. I need Your strength in my weakness. I need Your
love in my relationships. I need Your righteousness in
my sinfulness. I long to come to You and drink deeply.
In Jesus' name, amen.

Chapter Ten
When the Gospel Comes Home

The happiest times in my life were when my relationships
were going well—when I was in love with someone and someone
was loving me. But in my whole life, I haven't met the person I can
sustain a relationship with yet. So I'm discontented about that.
I'm angry with myself. I have regrets.
—Billy Joel, singer and songwriter

Over the years I have given hundreds of messages on a wide variety of themes—worship, prayer, the Holy Spirit, evangelism, ministry—but there is one theme in particular that always generates the most interest: relationships. We all long for deeper relationships and yet are often not really sure how to get there. While there are plenty of books and seminars offering principles for improved relationships, it doesn't take long to discover that trying hard to follow principles doesn't really touch the part of us through which healthy relationships happen: the heart. What has the power to change our hearts and thereby significantly impact our relationships?

Good News for Our Relationships

If you've made it this far in the book, I'm sure you instinctively know the answer to that question: the gospel. The gospel is the means whereby we experience healthy relationships. Don't believe me? Think about this: Have you ever noticed that whenever there is a significant discussion of relationships in the New Testament, it is almost always preceded by or rooted in a discussion of the gospel? In the book of 1 John, we find the continual encouragement to love each other flows from our experience of Christ's love for us: "We love because he first loved us" (1 John 4:19). The apostle Paul, while frequently dealing with the subject of relationships in his New Testament letters, never does so without first laying out the gospel. In the book of Colossians, for instance, his powerful discussion of relationships doesn't happen until chapter 3—after he has clearly explained the gospel. And then, when he finally does begin talking about relationships, notice how he introduces the subject: "*Therefore, as God's chosen people, holy and dearly loved*, clothe yourselves with compassion, kindness, humility, gentleness and patience" (Col. 3:12). He starts with the gospel! From Paul's perspective, our ability to demonstrate love in our relationships is rooted in the gospel. *Because* this is true of you—*because* you are dearly loved by God and completely accepted by Him through Jesus—you are freed to clothe yourselves in the compassion, patience, and gentleness of Christ.

Notice, it's not that we are generating these loving attributes from our own resources. We are instead choosing to be clothed in the resources of Christ. In other words, we are choosing to hear the melody of the gospel in our relationships. When I am in the midst of a situation in which everything within me wants to be impatient and say hurtful things to someone, I can at that moment embrace the gospel—acknowledging the depth of my self-centeredness and choosing to place my faith in Jesus, trusting Him to express His patience and kindness through me. Just think of the impact in all of your relationships as you choose to live the gospel moment by moment. The life of Christ will be poured into your spouse, your friends, your coworkers, your children. Such is the power of the gospel.

The Trajectory of the Gospel

I probably need to clarify something at this point. Yes, the gospel provides the *means* for us to more effectively love the people around us, but there is something else the gospel does as well: It *moves* us to love others. Love is the trajectory of the gospel. In the book of Galatians, after expounding on the nature of this incredible gospel, Paul says something absolutely fascinating: "The only thing that counts is faith expressing itself through love" (Gal. 5:6). The only thing that counts is faith, and the direct manifestation of that faith is love toward others. In other words, if we are not growing in our experience of love for others, we're not growing in our experience of the gospel. The natural trajectory of the gospel is outward. As we allow the gospel to more deeply penetrate our souls, it naturally and inevitably impacts the people around us.

Jesus uses a particular word to describe this manifestation of the gospel. In Matthew 5, as Jesus is explaining what it looks like to live in continual brokenness and faith, he says these words: "Blessed are the merciful, for they will be shown mercy" (Matt. 5:7). Now on the surface, this sounds as if God's mercy toward us depends on our demonstrating mercy toward others; as in, we earn God's mercy by being merciful. But that is the antithesis of the gospel, the antithesis of everything for which Jesus gave His life. So what is Jesus saying?

In this verse, Jesus makes a clear connection between *giving* mercy and *receiving* it. Merciful people are *able* to receive mercy from God, because they see their own need for mercy. Those who are merciful will receive mercy because their hearts are open to mercy. In contrast, people who are unmerciful toward others won't experience God's mercy. Why? Because they don't think they need it. Remember the story Jesus told in Luke 18 about the Pharisee going to the temple to pray? He thanked God that he wasn't like those sinful people—adulterers, tax collectors, and the like. After all, he regularly fasted and tithed. Here's a sincere, devout believer in God who has absolutely no capacity for mercy toward others. Why? Because his own heart is closed to mercy. He doesn't see his own desperate need for the mercy of God—and all of his relationships are crippled as a result.

When Mercy Comes to Church

There's actually an environment specifically designed for this mercy to be lived out and experienced—a safe context in which you can admit your weaknesses and your brokenness, receiving love and mercy from those around you. In turn, you are freed to extend that same mercy toward others who acknowledge their brokenness. Where is this relational environment? The body of Christ, commonly known as the church. In God's design, the church is not a building but a powerful context for life-giving relationships. Listen to Peter's description of the people of God in 1 Peter 2:

> As you come to him, the living Stone—rejected by men but chosen by God and precious to him—you also, like living stones, are being built into a spiritual house.... But you are a chosen people, a royal priesthood, a holy nation, a people belonging to God, that you may declare the praises of him who called you out of darkness into his wonderful light. Once you were not a people, but now you are the people of God; once you had not received mercy, but now you have received mercy. (1 Peter 2:4–5, 9–10)

Peter is describing the fact that when we enter into a relationship with God through the gospel, we are at that moment placed into a spiritual family, united with others who also belong to God because of the gospel. Notice one of the defining characteristics of this spiritual family: mercy. "Now you have received mercy." The church family is to be a context for mercy to be experienced. But has this been your church experience? Is mercy an evident part of the atmosphere in most churches?

A Christian friend of mine was attending Al-Anon meetings to help herself deal with the issue of alcohol abuse in her family. There were two meetings that she could attend—one was made up of believers on her Christian college campus, the other composed of

nonbelievers in the community. Any idea which meeting she pre-
ferred? The one with nonbelievers. Why? She told me that in the
Christian meeting, she didn't feel safe sharing honestly about her
brokenness and pain. There was an underlying and unspoken message that permeated the meeting: *Mature* Christians don't struggle.
The result was a superficiality in which no one dared admit his or her
brokenness. Mercy was nowhere to be found. Ironically and sadly,
she experienced more mercy at the other meeting, where people
freely shared about their own struggles.

I believe this describes the unspoken reality in many churches.
We may talk from the pulpit about mercy, but do people really feel
safe in sharing honestly about their own struggles with sin, depres-
sion, fear? Is it okay in the church to admit you've had an abortion
or that you struggle with an eating disorder or that your marriage is
devoid of any emotional intimacy or that you haven't had a prayer
time alone with the Lord in months? Is it okay to be real? There
is a yearning in our hearts to be open and honest with our brothers and sisters in Christ. However, when we wade into the water of
authenticity, we are often met with blank stares and silence or with
superficial platitudes and stern lectures. We soon learn that it's better
to keep this stuff to ourselves. So we come to church or our small
groups with a smile painted on our face, making sure no one sees any
evidence of the brokenness lying just below the surface.

Mercy Deficit

Why is it in the church we struggle so much in being real with
one another? Why is it our relationships are so often characterized
by flattery and superficiality rather than honest engagement and

speaking the truth in love? It goes back to Jesus' words in Matthew 5:7: "Blessed are the merciful, for they will be shown mercy." Those who are unable to give mercy to others are often people who are unable to truly receive it from God. They are not experiencing the depths of God's mercy at the core of their beings. In other words, they're not hearing the melody of the gospel, and it's significantly impacting their relationships.

When the people of God lose sight of the gospel—when the underlying message is focused on pursuing principles and trying harder to please God—the church family becomes a breeding ground for all sorts of relational viruses: self-sufficiency, pride, a critical spirit, a lack of compassion. We feel a need to hide behind our religious performance for fear of being found out. *If they really knew the struggles in my life, they would reject me.* This was Adam and Eve's instinctive response in Genesis 3 after giving in to sin and experiencing the awful pain of guilt and shame. They hid—not only from God—but also from each other. Well aware of their reality, they instinctively tried to make it look like they had it all together—and we've been doing the same thing ever since. Churches are often filled with Christians who are trying so hard to cover themselves in order not to be discovered.

However, when a church body clearly and continually embraces the gospel, people are freed by the life-giving power of mercy to move *toward* others in loving relationships. If deep in our souls we are experiencing the mercy of Jesus loving us in our brokenness, we no longer have to hide. We no longer have to pretend that we're doing great. We no longer have to remain behind the veneer of superspirituality and having it all together. To live the gospel is to admit you don't have it all together. A pastor friend of mine likes to state it this way: "I'm not okay. You're not okay. And that's okay."

Now you may be thinking that this sounds like I'm encouraging everyone to simply wallow together in their sin. But in reality, the opposite actually happens. When our sin is removed from that place of secrecy and shame and is suddenly brought into the atmosphere of mercy extended to us from brothers and sisters in Christ, it begins to lose some of its power in our lives. Perhaps this is what James is referring to in James 5:16 when he says, "Confess your sins *to each other* and pray for each other so that you may be healed." It is in the prayerful admission of our sin *to one another* that healing can take place—a healing of our isolation, our self-sufficiency, our independence. Such is the power of mercy in our lives. It frees us to move toward others in love.

A few years ago, I realized that this kind of relational engagement was not as much a part of my life as it needed to be. It was too easy for me to hide what was really going on in my life. So I invited three other pastors in town to meet monthly for two hours. I made it clear from the start that our agenda was not Bible study or theological debate. Rather, our primary objective was to create a safe context where we could be honest about what was really going on in our lives and our souls. I'm not sure any of us realized how life changing this would be. As we have opened our hearts to each other, admitting personal struggles with anything from parenting to pornography, the power of mercy has been overwhelming and transformational. Each one of us has, at one time or another, freely admitted we're not sure where our lives and ministries would be today without this group. Sin thrives in secret, but in the context of authentic, mercy-filled relationships, it loosens its grip as the gospel increasingly takes hold.

What I've learned from this experience is that the melody of the gospel is most clearly heard in the context of authentic relationships, where we can be brutally honest about our brokenness and can encourage one another in our lives of faith. We need each other in our gospel journeys. Perhaps this is why the church is such an important part of God's plan. A church family fully embracing the gospel becomes an environment in which mercy can breathe life into our relationships and into our souls. But it doesn't stop there. The power of mercy is such that it is to extend beyond ourselves and our churches as it significantly impacts the world.

Mercy in the World

Do you remember the television sitcom *Cheers*? The entire show was built upon the relational interaction between the regulars who hung out together at a Boston bar. While I have forgotten most of the episodes, I have never forgotten the theme song that every week was used to start the show:

Sometimes you want to go where everybody knows your name

And they're always glad you came.

You want to be where you can see,

Your troubles are all the same.[1]

There is something within every human heart that longs for a place to belong, a place where we can take off our masks and be ourselves, a place where we can be honest about our struggles. Everyone I've ever met feels this same yearning.

Now as we just discussed, the gospel enables the church family to be such a place—to be a place where authentic relationships can happen, where mercy can be experienced. But this raises an obvious question: Does the world view the church as this kind of place? I've seen a number of surveys and man-on-the-street interviews in which people are asked to describe Christians. Strangely absent from the responses are words like *mercy* and *compassion*. Instead, we often hear things like *hypocritical, judgmental, narrow, condescending, angry, hateful.* Why is that? Seriously. Why are we better known for our boycotts and angry letters to the editor than for our mercy?

My hunch is that we are not comfortable extending mercy because we are not comfortable receiving it. We prefer to think of ourselves as *deserving* recipients of God's mercy rather than undeserving sinners continually in need of it. Could this be why it seems so few people in America are really interested in the gospel we are offering? While we certainly *believe* in mercy, our lives often communicate a different reality. When we are not drinking deeply of Christ's mercy, we end up looking at the world as the enemy and treating lost people as outsiders.

In our heart of hearts, we can easily look with disdain at people living immoral lifestyles. If we do reach out, the message is often, "Here, let us help you get your life cleaned up." Quick translation: "Our lives are cleaned up, and we can help you clean up yours." Is that the gospel? No. The gospel of the kingdom says to the world, "Look, I'm broken just like you. You are looking for life in a homosexual relationship or in alcohol. I'm often looking for life in my money or my success—but we both struggle with the same root problem. We are both trying to find life in something other than God."

The truth is this: All have sinned. All are in need of God's mercy—that "all" includes you and me. We can't offer the world a gospel that we ourselves are not experiencing. If we try, it will come off as being shallow and inauthentic. We will simply be offering propositional facts to believe or a formula to get to heaven rather than offering them the person of Jesus—the same person of whom we are drinking so deeply.

In our brokenness we offer the world a much more powerful gospel than we do in our strength. The gospel allows us to *feel* the world's brokenness rather than trying to run from it. The gospel frees us to ask questions and listen rather than simply talking to be heard. The gospel unleashes in us a desire to love sinners just as we are loved by God as sinners. The more deeply we experience the gospel, the more significant our impact for Christ will be.

The Power of Mercy

In his book *Blue Like Jazz,* Donald Miller tells about an experience he had in college that captures the profound impact of mercy. Each year, the students on his campus would celebrate a festival called Ren Fair in which the entire campus was shut down for the weekend so that students could party freely. Miller's small group of Christian friends found themselves discussing how they could make an impact for Christ during the festival. After one person jokingly suggested having a confession booth set up in the middle of campus for people to confess their sins, a radical idea began to take shape: Why not have a confession booth where, instead of receiving confessions, *we* confess to them our shortcomings as followers of Christ?

So they built this confession booth in the middle of campus and put out a sign that read "Confess your sins." No one went in during the day or evening on Saturday, but since the party went all night, they kept the booth open. Finally, in the early morning hours, they received their first customer. A guy named Jake walked in and expected to confess his sins, but the booth didn't live up to his expectations. What Jake found was Miller and his friends wanting to confess the ways in which Christians have not represented Jesus very well. After the initial shock and laughter, Jake suddenly got serious and asked Miller what he was confessing.

> "There's a lot," I said. "I will keep it short…. Jesus said to feed the poor and to heal the sick. I have never done very much about that. Jesus said to love those who persecute me. I tend to lash out, especially if I feel threatened, you know, if my ego gets threatened. Jesus did not mix His spirituality with politics. I grew up doing that. It got in the way of the central message of Christ. I know that was wrong and I know that a lot of people will not listen to the words of Christ because people like me, who know Him, carry our own agendas into the conversation rather than just relaying the message Christ wanted us to get across. There's a lot more, you know."
>
> "It's all right, man," Jake said, very tenderly. His eyes were starting to water.
>
> "Well," I said…. "I'm sorry for all of that."
>
> "I forgive you," Jake said. And he meant it. "You really believe in Jesus, don't you?" He asked me.

"Yes, I think I do.… I have doubts at times but mostly I believe in Him."

He then asked, "You said earlier that there was a central message of Christ. I don't really want to become a Christian, you know, but what is that message?"

"The message is that man sinned against God and God gave the world over to man, and that if somebody wanted to be rescued out of that, if somebody for instance finds it all very empty, that Christ will rescue them if they want.… What do you believe about God?"

"I don't know. I believe somebody is responsible for all of this.… It is all very confusing."

"Jake, if you want to know God, you can. I'm just saying that if you ever want to call on Jesus, He will be there."

"Thanks, man. I believe that you mean that." His eyes were watering again. "This is cool what you guys are doing," he repeated. "I'm going to tell my friends about this."

He shook my hand, and when he left the booth there was somebody else ready to get in. It went like that for a couple of hours. I talked to about thirty people.… Many people wanted to hug when we were done. All of the people who visited the booth were grateful and gracious. I was being changed through the process.[2]

That's what the gospel does the more fully we embrace it—it changes us. It frees us. We are freed to admit our brokenness and embrace our Savior. We are freed to love others. And we are freed to impact the world.

For Personal Reflection/Response

- Say the word *mercy* aloud, and then write down the first five words that come to mind. Does your list accurately reflect God's mercy, or is it something distorted?

- Who is one person you can extend mercy to this week? As you prepare for this, mentally walk through that scenario in your mind and heart, and then invite Jesus into it, even before it happens.

- What is one area of your own life you can extend mercy to this week? (This may seem or feel a bit awkward, but remember, if you cannot accept God's mercy toward yourself, then it's probably going to be difficult to extend it to others.)

✳ ✳ ✳

*Heavenly Father, thank You for Your mercy that
is mine through the gospel. I confess I need to hear the
melody of mercy more deeply in my soul. I too easily hide
who I really am and in turn look down on others who
I perceive are worse off than me. Set me free to
experience Your mercy and in turn extend it to others.
In Jesus' name, amen.*

Epilogue

One of my favorite images of this gospel life God invites us to experience is found in a vision the prophet Ezekiel receives. He sees a river flowing from God's throne and immediately realizes this is no ordinary stream.

> Swarms of living creatures will live wherever the river flows. There will be large numbers of fish, because this water flows there and makes the salt water fresh; so where the river flows everything will live.... Fruit trees of all kinds will grow on both banks of the river. Their leaves will not wither, nor will their fruit fail. Every month they will bear, because the water from the sanctuary flows to them. Their fruit will serve for food and their leaves for healing. (Ezek. 47:9, 12)

This is the river of God's purposes, a river that brings life into places of barrenness, fruitfulness into places of drought. It is the healing stream of the gospel of the kingdom, an amazing and beautiful picture of what God desires to do in the world. But there is something even more fascinating that happens in this passage. Ezekiel is actually invited by God to *wade into* this life-giving stream.

> As the man went eastward with a measuring line in his hand, he measured off a thousand cubits and then led me through water that was ankle-deep. He measured off another thousand cubits and led me through water that was knee-deep. He measured off another thousand and led me through water that was up to the waist. He measured off another thousand, but now it was a river that I could not cross, because the water had risen and was deep enough to swim in—a river that no one could cross. (Ezek. 47:3–5)

What an awesome picture of our involvement in God's purposes! The powerful river of His gospel is flowing freely, bringing healing and life to any who embrace it. We who have embraced this glorious gospel are standing in ankle-deep water, enjoying the stream. But soon God opens our eyes to see that if we go out a little farther, this water rises to our knees and then to our waists. Now let's take this out of the theoretical and into the realm of reality: Imagine yourself wading into a powerful river that's flowing by. At first you are ankle-deep, but then you begin to wade out farther into knee-deep and then waist-high water. What happens to you the farther you wade into the river? The force of the river begins to exert more influence. Suddenly you are fearful at your lack of control, and yet the exhilaration of the water invites you to go deeper.

This is the journey of the gospel as we experience deeper levels of brokenness and faith. We see in increasing ways our own inadequacy, and we find ourselves embracing a power that is beyond anything we have experienced. Very soon, we realize this river is much deeper than our waists. It is actually deep enough in which to swim. It's a bit scary, and yet as we increasingly let go of our self-effort and control, we are enveloped in the raging and wild current of an all-sufficient and glorious Savior who loves us passionately and longs for the world to experience this as well. Don't settle for an ankle-deep experience of the gospel—a wearying Christianity in which you get a little bit of Jesus and a whole lot of self-effort. Go for a swim. Freely and continually admit how desperately you need Him, and then wholeheartedly dive into Jesus, who is your life. Embrace the adventure of living the gospel. Your life will never be the same.

Notes

Chapter 1

1. As quoted in *Sonship,* 2nd ed. (Jenkintown, PA: World Harvest Mission, 2002), 25.

Chapter 2

1. Another example of this can be found in Jeremiah 3:12–13, where God urges His people to "return" (same Hebrew word as *repent*). He then describes this repentance in more detail: "Only acknowledge your guilt" (Jer. 3:13). That word *acknowledge* is the Hebrew word *yada,* which means "to know intimately." God realizes that our repenting is rooted in our "knowing intimately" our sin, in other words truly *seeing* the guilt of our sin.

2. John Stott, *The Cross of Christ* (Downers Grove, IL: InterVarsity, 1986), 160.

3. As quoted in *Gospel Transformation*, 2nd ed. (Jenkintown, PA: World Harvest Mission, 2006), 40.

4. As quoted in Dwight Edwards, *Revolution Within* (Colorado Springs: WaterBrook, 2001), 43.

Chapter 3

1. As quoted in *Readers Digest*, September 2007, 111.

2. Henri Nouwen, *The Return of the Prodigal Son* (New York: Doubleday, 1994), 71–72.

3. Ibid., 72.

Chapter 4

1. Gary Smalley, *Joy That Lasts* (Grand Rapids, MI: Zondervan, 1988), 78–80.

2. C. S. Lewis, *Mere Christianity* (New York: Macmillan, 1952), 109.

Chapter 5

1. Still not convinced? Check out these Scriptures: Romans 3:21–28; 14:23; 2 Corinthians 5:7; 10:15; Galatians 5:6; Ephesians 3:16–17; Philippians 3:7–10; Colossians 2:6–7; 1 Thessalonians 1:3; 2 Thessalonians 1:11; 1 Timothy 1:5; Hebrews 11:1–40.

2. From *The Fellowship of the Ring* movie based on novel by J. R. R. Tolkien. Movie screenplay written by Peter Jackson, Fran Walsh, and Philippa Boyens. Transcript found at www.council-of-elrond.com/fotrse.html (accessed June 18, 2008).

3. Also described in Bill Thrall, Bruce McNicol, and John Lynch, *TrueFaced: Experience Edition* (Colorado Springs: NavPress, 2004), 37–56.

Chapter 6

1. V. Raymond Edman, *They Found the Secret* (Grand Rapids, MI: Zondervan, 1984), 2.

2. Ibid., 3.

3. While the Sabbath in the Old Testament was on Saturday, New Testament believers began celebrating the Sabbath on Sunday because of Jesus' resurrection being on Sunday.

Chapter 7

1. The "law" in this passage represents God's revealed truth to us, i.e., the Bible.

Chapter 8

1. Brennan Manning, *The Wisdom of Tenderness* (New York: Harper-Collins, 2002), 25–26. As quoted in Edward Farrell, *The Father Is Very Fond of Me* (Denville, NJ: Dimension, 1978).
2. C. S. Lewis, *The Weight of Glory* (Grand Rapids, MI: Eerdmans, 1975), 12–13.

Chapter 9

1. David Eckman, *Becoming Who God Intended* (Eugene, OR: Harvest House, 2005), 199–202.
2. John F. Smeltzer, "Journey Out of Religiosity" paper, pp. 18–19 (used with permission).
3. This phrase comes from Brother Lawrence, a monk who lived in the seventeenth century. His letters have been published under the title *The Practice of the Presence of God*. They are public domain on various Web sites.
4. Now sometimes Christians freak out about this kind of thing and reject it for fear of "New Age" influences. While I appreciate the concern, we also must remember that part of the Spirit's ministry in our lives is to help us *experience* the presence of Jesus. Paul freely

talks about "the fellowship of the Spirit" that is ours to enjoy (see Phil. 2:1; 2 Cor. 13:14). What is "fellowship" if it doesn't include a real encounter with the presence of Christ?

5. As described in Richard Foster and James Bryan Smith, eds., *Devotional Classics* (New York: HarperCollins, 1993), 94.

Chapter 10

1. "Where Everybody Knows Your Name" © Gary Portnoy and Judy Hart Angelo, 1982.

2. Donald Miller, *Blue Like Jazz* (Nashville, TN: Thomas Nelson, 2003), 113–27.